TOP**10**
COPENHAGEN

Top 10 Copenhagen Highlights

The Top 10 of Everything

CONTENTS

Copenhagen
Area by Area

Streetsmart

Within each Top 10 list in this book, no hierarchy of quality or popularity is implied. All 10 are, in the editor's opinion, of roughly equal merit.

Title page, front cover and spine
Boats moored at colourful Nyhavn
Back cover, clockwise from top left
A traditional Dutch sandwich; Amagertorv town square; Nyhavn in the evening; Nyhavn waterfront; Sunset in the Old Town

Welcome to
Copenhagen

Welcome to Copenhagen, the cultural capital of northern Europe and birthplace of hygge. A charming, compact city where opulent palaces stand shoulder to shoulder with modern architectural masterpieces, the Danish capital can be experienced in a multitude of different ways. With Eyewitness Top 10 Copenhagen, it's yours to explore.

Copenhagen has royal credentials that are clear the moment you set foot on the city's cobblestone streets, with magnificent palaces, castles and churches dominating the skyline. But even with its regal past (it's home to the world's oldest monarchy) casting a long shadow, Copenhagen remains a dynamic, modern city with much to offer to even the most museum-wary traveller – from world-class restaurants, hip nightlife and high-end boutiques to breathtaking parks, urban beaches and cosy cafés.

It's no coincidence that Denmark is often cited as the happiest nation on earth. Danes may be direct – and their humour dry – but they know better than most how to enjoy the finer things in life. After all, hygge – the Danish lifestyle trend that loosely translates into a feeling of warmth and cosiness – is now almost as popular outside of Denmark as one of the country's other great exports: beer.

Whether you're visiting for a weekend or a week, our Top 10 guide brings together the best of everything the city has to offer, from vibrant **Vesterbro** to stately **Slotsholmen** and beyond. The guide gives you useful tips throughout, from seeking out what's free to avoiding the crowds, plus seven easy-to-follow itineraries, designed to tie together a clutch of sights in a short space of time. Add inspiring photography and detailed maps, and you've got the essential pocket-sized travel companion. **Enjoy the book, and enjoy Copenhagen.**

Clockwise from top: Christiansborg Slot, the interior of Grundtvigs Kirke, houses on Nyhavn, the Frederiksborg Slot gardens, ceiling of Marmorkirken dome, Amalienborg sentries, street art in Christiania

Exploring Copenhagen

Copenhagen may not be the biggest of capital cities, but it punches well above its weight in terms of culture, history and charm. Despite its compact size, there is a lot to see and do. To help you make the most of your visit, here are some ideas for a two- or four-day trip.

Christiansborg Slot has magnificent interiors.

Key
— Two-day itinerary
— Four-day itinerary

Nyhavn is a waterfront entertainment area.

Two Days in Copenhagen

Day ❶
MORNING

Set sail from **Nyhavn** *(see pp22–3)* on a canal tour, then stroll along the promenade past the Royal Danish Playhouse. Follow the harbourside path until you reach **Amalienborg** *(see pp24–5)*, where you can watch the changing of the guard. Have lunch at **Kompasset** *(see p75)*.

AFTERNOON

Head west on Gothersgade until you reach **Kongens Have** *(see pp16–17)*. Stroll through the gardens, then continue to **Rosenborg Slot** *(see pp16–17)* to see the crown jewels. Walk north on Øster Voldgade and visit **SMK – National Gallery of Denmark** *(see pp26–7)*, ending the afternoon with a drink at **Torvehallerne KBH** *(see p63)*.

Day ❷
MORNING

Begin the day at **Nationalmuseet** *(see pp32–3)*, making sure to visit the Viking exhibition. Next, go to **Slotsholmen** *(see pp30–31)* and visit the Royal Stables before taking a tour of the Royal Reception Rooms at Christiansborg Slot. Climb the palace tower for amazing views. Stop at the Tower Restaurant for an innovative spin on a *smørrebrød* (open sandwich).

AFTERNOON

Head southwest on Stormgade to **Ny Carlsberg Glyptotek** *(see p70)*, before crossing Tietgensgade and exploring **Tivoli** *(see pp14–15)*. After spending a couple of hours here, exit onto Vesterbrogade and walk east towards the **Latin Quarter** *(see pp18–19)* for sightseeing and shops.

Four Days in Copenhagen

Day ❶
MORNING

Make **SMK – National Gallery of Denmark** *(see pp26–7)* your first stop of the day, then cross Georg Brandes Plads and head to **Rosenborg Slot** *(see pp16–17)*. Take a guided tour of

0 metres 800
0 yards 800

Day ❸

MORNING

Start the day with a trip to **Zoologisk Have** (see p88), and visit the elephant house here. Stroll through **Frederiksberg Have** (see p87) before exiting onto Pile Alle. Pass under the elephant gate and make your way into **Visit Carlsberg** (see p88).

AFTERNOON

Stroll northeast and stop at **Bakkehuset** (see p89). Turn right to get onto Vesterbrogade and call in at **Sønder Boulevard** (see p89) for a late lunch. Continue on Vesterbrogade and turn right onto Gasværksvej, following the road until you reach Kødbyen, where you will find a plethora of trendy bars.

the 17th-century palace before exiting into **Kongens Have** (see pp16–17). Head east to **Marmorkirken**, and then on to **Amalienborg** (see pp24–5). Stop at **Ida Davidsen** (see p83) for lunch.

AFTERNOON

Walk west, stopping to admire the Gefionspringvandet and St Alban's Church before crossing the footbridge into **Kastellet** (see p80). See the **Little Mermaid** (see p80) from the fortress ramparts, then catch a 1A bus into **Kongens Nytorv** (see pp22–3). Stroll along Strøget, then have a drink at one of Amagertorv's cafés.

Day ❷

MORNING

Start the day at **Nationalmuseet** (see pp32–3) and museum-hop on **Slotsholmen** (see pp30–31) before popping into the Royal Stables. Take a torchlit tour of the ruins under Christiansborg Slot.

AFTERNOON

Cross the **harbour** (see pp12–13) and enter Christianshavn. Turn right to visit the **Christians Kirke** (see p93) on Strandgade, then head east until you reach the canal, crossing the bridge on Sankt Annæ Gade and arrive at **Vor Frelsers Kirke** (see p94). Spend the afternoon in **Christiania** (see pp28–9).

Day ❹

MORNING

Begin the day with a coffee at one of the many cafés along Studiestræde before exploring into the bustling **Latin Quarter** (see pp18–19). Head up Store Kannikestræde to Rundtårn, and then hike to the top. Continue into **Nyhavn** (see pp22–3) for lunch.

AFTERNOON

Take a boat tour of the canals and jump off at **Holmens Kirke** (see p41). Walk west along Gammel Strand, passing **Rådhus** (see p70) before turning onto Vesterbrogade. Take a left into **Tivoli** (see pp14–15), and spend the afternoon wandering the beautiful 19th-century pleasure gardens.

Tivoli Gardens has manicured lawns, flowers and fountains.

Top 10 Copenhagen Highlights

Fishing boats on the water in the
historic district of Nyhavn

TOP 10 Copenhagen Highlights

Copenhagen is a vibrant city offering an array of experiences. Walk through the cobbled streets of the medieval city, explore world-class museums, experience the finest restaurants and hippest nightlife, or simply unwind beside the gorgeous waters of one of the nearby peaceful seaside towns. This charming destination has something for everyone.

1 Harbour Sights

The best way to soak up Copenhagen's harbour sights is to take a boat trip along the canals of Slotsholmen and Christianshavn. It is also a good way to understand the city's development (see pp12–13).

2 Tivoli

This pleasure garden and funfair attracts kids and adults. The rides are great for an adrenaline rush, and if you feel peckish there are many restaurants (see pp14–15).

3 Rosenborg Slot and Kongens Have

Set in one of the city's prettiest parks, the lovely 17th-century Rosenborg Castle houses the royal regalia, including the dazzling Crown Jewels (see p16).

4 Latin Quarter

One of the oldest areas in Copenhagen, the Latin Quarter is just off the main pedestrianized street, Strøget (see pp18–19).

5 Kongens Nytorv and Nyhavn

Kongens Nytorv (King's New Square) is a splendid Baroque square at the top of Nyhavn. Previously a seedy haunt for sailors, Nyhavn has been radically transformed. It is now a waterside attraction with bars and restaurants (see pp22–3).

6 Amalienborg and Frederiksstaden

Home to the royal family since 1794, this complex of palaces represents some of the best Rococo architecture in Denmark, plus fascinating displays *(see pp24–5)*.

7 SMK – National Gallery of Denmark

You will find a wonderful collection of Danish and European sculpture as well as paintings at the SMK. It is housed in a beautiful 19th-century building, connected by a glass bridge to a modern wing *(see pp26–7)*.

8 Christiania

This is a wonderland of cafés, bars, music venues, art galleries and fiercely independent shops – and a must-see for anyone interested in the city's thriving counter-culture *(see pp28–9)*.

10 Nationalmuseet

Here is a perfect example of how brilliantly the Danes design their museums. You will find some fabulous ethnographic artifacts from around the world, as well as an excellent children's museum *(see pp32–3)*.

9 Slotsholmen

This is where it all began in the 12th century. The present Neo-Baroque castle was built in 1907–28, but was never inhabited by the monarch. It is shared between the royals and Parliament *(see pp30–31)*.

Harbour Sights

A harbour tour is a delightful way to take in the city's brilliant views and varied topography. You will be taken along the wide waters of the Inner Harbour and winding waterways of Christianshavn, then round to Slotsholmen (the island on which the original town of Havn flourished in the 12th century). Vor Frelsers Kirke, in particular, makes a spectacular sight as you look up through the rigging of sailing boats dotting the Christianshavn canal.

1 The Canals
The canals that you glide along on the tour (above) were built in a Dutch style in 1618 at the command of Christian IV. It is because of this that Christianshavn is referred to as "Little Amsterdam".

2 Operaen
The Opera House (below) was built in just four years. Its massive, orange-maple coloured auditorium seats 1,700 people (see pp94–5). The foyer's sculptures change colour with the weather.

3 Vor Frelsers Kirke
With a soaring twisted spire, this opulent church dominates the Christianshavn skyline. An ascent offers an unparalleled vantage point over the city.

4 Nyhavn
Even today, the utterly charming old harbour of Nyhavn is filled with boats. The old brothels and pubs have now been turned into respectable bars and restaurants serving good, traditional Danish dishes.

5 Den Sorte Diamant
The Black Diamond, a vast, eye-catching structure, holds all the books ever published in Denmark (see p64). It is the largest library in the Nordic countries, and a great place to find original Danish texts.

7 Havnebadet
Take a refreshing dip in the sparkling clean harbour waters **(left)** of this popular open-air pool *(see p49)*, while enjoying superb views of the city. There are three pools to choose from – for adults, for children and a smaller pool for divers.

8 Langelinie
One of the city's most scenic areas, this is a wonderful place to walk along the harbour banks. Stroll along, past Kastellet and the Little Mermaid, right up to the final stretch where there is a cruise ship terminal.

MUTANT MERMAID

Set close to the Little Mermaid, and almost inviting controversy, is a sculpture group called *Paradise Genetically Altered* by Danish artist Bjørn Nørgaard. There is a triumphal arch, with a 9-m (29-ft) genetically altered Madonna atop it, surrounded by figures of Adam, Eve, Christ, Mary Magdalene, the Tripartite Capital – a critical representation of capitalism – and a pregnant man. On its own small island not far away sits the *Genetically Modified Little Mermaid*.

9 The Little Mermaid
Den Lille Havfrue is a surprisingly small landmark, ordered by brewery magnate Carl Jacobsen in 1909 as a gift to the city of Copenhagen. It was created in 1913 *(see p80)* by Edvard Eriksen, whose wife, Eline, was the model.

10 Pavilions and the Royal Yacht
On the quayside, just beyond the Little Mermaid, are two green-domed pavilions. It is here that the Danish royal family gathers before boarding their stunning 79-m (259-ft) royal yacht, called the *Dannebrog* **(right)**, which shares its name with the Danish flag (said to have fallen from the sky in the year 1219).

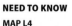

Harbour Sights

6 Houseboats
The houseboats along the canals range from boat-like structures to some with barge-like designs, and other homes built on floating platforms, complete with outdoor spaces.

NEED TO KNOW

MAP L4

■ Both Stromma and Netto Boats offer guided canal and harbour tours *(see p109)*.

■ The tours run daily round the year, with several departures per day.

■ Public buses whose routes run along the harbour include the 901 and 902 from Den Sorte Diamant, Nyhavn, Knippelsbro, Operaen, Nyholm or Larsen Plads.

■ Buses 991, 992 and 993 run between Refshaleøen (Holmen) and Langelinie. Copenhagen Cards *(see p112)* are also accepted.

TOP 10 ⭐ Tivoli

Famous for its magical fairy-tale ambience, exotic buildings, gorgeous landscaped gardens and upmarket entertainment and restaurants, Tivoli Gardens is more than an amusement park. The atmosphere is magical enough to merit a visit even if you are not interested in the excellent rides on offer. Founded in 1843, Tivoli has long been a favourite with royalty. It also proved to be a great source of inspiration for Walt Disney, who visited in the 1950s and is said to have been fascinated by Tivoli's atmosphere.

2 Thrill Rides

Day or night, Tivoli rings with the shrieks of people whizzing along on thrill rides such as *Aquila*, *The Demon* **(left)**, *Vertigo* and *The Starflyer*, which reaches a height of 80 m (262 ft).

1 Gentle Rides

For children and the faint-hearted, there are plenty of fun, gentle rides. The Ferris wheel is an observation wheel that offers great views over Tivoli. You could also enjoy a trolley-bus ride, a carousel ride with exotic animals and music, a waltzer in the shape of a pirate ship and several charming kids' rides, such as flying dragons and miniature classic cars.

3 Tivoli Concert Hall and Open-Air Stage

The hall hosts varied performances. There is music daily in the Harmony Pavilion, and free rock concerts on Friday nights (May–Sep).

4 Pantomime Theatre

Built in 1874, this theatre **(below)** has an exotic Chinese design and a spectacular stage curtain styled like a peacock's tail. It is known for its very enjoyable mime shows.

5 Dragon Boats

These boats **(above)** are very popular rides at Tivoli. Kids love floating on the lake during the day. In the evenings, the setting turns romantic.

6 Tivoli at Night

At night Tivoli is utterly magical, sparkling resplendently with thousands of fairy lights and Chinese lanterns. You can catch the dazzling Tivoli Illuminations over the lake, an exuberant, late-night show with fireworks, lasers, music and waterjets.

7 Traditional Rides

Tivoli's current Ferris wheel dates from 1943. The Roller Coaster **(left)** was built in 1914 and is one of the oldest of its kind. It reaches speeds of 58 kmph (36 mph). The classic carousel is also very popular, perfect for adults looking for a dose of nostalgia.

CHRISTMAS AT TIVOLI

For six weeks between mid-November and the end of December Tivoli transforms into a winter wonderland: an exciting, no-holds-barred, Father Christmas-strewn, elf-driven, illuminated extravaganza that you and the kids aren't likely to forget in a hurry!

8 Tivoli Akvarium

Don't miss the amazing aquarium in the foyer of the Concert Hall. Based on a tropical coral reef, this extensive salt-water aquarium is home to more than 1,600 fish of over 500 varieties. Among the popular attractions are the eels.

9 Tivoli Youth Guard

A tradition since 1844, the Youth Guard parades through Tivoli – complete with instruments, coach and horses – forming a delightful picture.

NEED TO KNOW

MAP H5

■ Vesterbrogade 3 ■ 33 15 10 01 ■ www.tivoli.dk

Open summer: 11am–11pm Sun–Thu (until midnight Fri & Sat); winter: 11am–9pm Sun–Thu (until 10pm Fri & Sat; hours can vary, check website before visiting)

Adm varies (check website for details)

■ Go on the thrill rides during the day, as long queues can build up in the evenings.

10 Nimb Hotel

This splendid hotel **(below)**, housed in the Nimb building, offers a variety of culinary experiences, such as a *vinoteque*, the Cakenhagen (bakery), a Bar'n'Grill with primed steaks and a brasserie.

TOP 10 ⭐ Rosenborg Slot and Kongens Have

Rosenborg Castle was originally built as a summer house in 1606–34 by Christian IV. At that time, it stood surrounded by sprawling gardens (now the Kongens Have park) out in the tranquil countryside. This was Christian IV's favourite castle, and many rooms retain the original Renaissance decor from his residency. When he was on his deathbed at Frederiksborg Castle in 1648, he insisted on being brought to Rosenborg Castle, and eventually died here.

1 Knight's Hall
Known as the Long Hall before 1750, this room (above) was completed in 1624 as a celebration hall. Only two Dutch fireplaces still remain from its original elaborate decorations.

2 Royal Residence
Complete with fairy-tale turrets and bronze lions guarding the entrance (below), the castle is wholly regal. In 1838, it became the first royal residence to open to the public.

3 Marble Hall
Originally serving as the bedroom of Kirsten Munk, Christian IV's morganatic wife, this room was turned into a Baroque show of splendour to celebrate the Absolute Monarchy.

4 Crown Jewels
The castle has been used as the treasury of the realm since 1658. In the castle's heavily guarded basement are Denmark's Crown Jewels (above).

5 Dark Room
This room is filled with fascinating objects, such as wax portraits of Frederik III and a 17th-century trick chair.

⑧ Frederik IV's Chamber Room

In the 1700s, this room **(above)** was used by Frederik IV's sister as an antechamber and the tapestries that hang here date back to this period. Note the intricate equestrian silver statue of Frederik. The coffered ceiling is the original.

⑨ Christian IV's Bedroom

Another private royal apartment, this room contains Christian IV's bloodied clothing, from the naval battle of Kolberger Heide (1644) where he lost an eye. The king wanted these clothes preserved as national mementos.

⑩ Winter Room

This panelled room **(below)** is said to have been one of Christian IV's most important private chambers. Look out for the speaking tubes that connect with the wine cellar and room above.

⑥ Glass Cabinet

This room was designed as a glass cabinet in 1713–14 by Frederik IV. The cabinet was built to house the extensive collection of glassware presented to Frederik in 1709 by the city of Venice, and its contents are amazing.

⑦ Kongens Have

Visited by over 2 million people every year, these are Denmark's oldest royal gardens and date back to the 17th century. There is a rose garden, which contains many statues. Various art events and a puppet theatre for children are held during summer.

⭐ Latin Quarter

The Latin Quarter is home to Copenhagen's university, where Latin used to be the spoken language. One of the oldest areas in the city, it is full of 17th-century buildings that were built by the architect king, Christian IV. Although there have been dwellings here since medieval times, most of them were destroyed in the disastrous fire that spread across Copenhagen in 1728. Today, the Latin Quarter is a lively and bustling student area brimming with shops and cafés.

Højbro Plads ①

The 1902 bronze equestrian statue **(right)** on this popular square depicts the 12th-century Bishop Absalon, founder of Copenhagen, facing the site of his original castle on Slotsholmen.

② Sankt Petri Kirke

Older than Vor Frue Kirke, Copenhagen's German church also suffered from city fires and the British bombardment of 1807 (see p39). Its vaulted sepulchral chapel has monuments and tombs dating back to 1681.

⑤ Rundetårn

The Round Tower (see p46) was built in 1642 by Christian IV as an observatory, its official role until 1861. It is 34.8 m (114 ft) high, with an internal ramp that spirals almost to the top. It holds art exhibitions and concerts in the library.

Latin Quarter

*(Map labels: NINA BANGS PLADS, KRYSTALGADE, STORE KANNIKESTR., KØBMAGERGADE, PILESTRÆDE, NØRREGADE, SKINDERGADE, N. HEMMINGSENS G., STRØGET, GAMMEL-TORV, HØJBRO PLADS)*

③ Regensen

This 17th-century student residence lies opposite the Rundetårn. A part of it burned down in the great fire of 1728, but was soon rebuilt. Its students retain the old tradition of "storming" Rundetårn every May.

④ Gråbrødretorv

Named after the Grey Brothers who built Copenhagen's first monastery here, this lovely 13th-century square **(right)** is now a popular place for locals and visitors to enjoy alfresco meals or drinks.

7 Trinitatis Kirke

This magnificent church **(left)** was built in 1637–56 for the staff and students of the university *(see p38)*. If it happens to be closed when you visit, you can enter Rundetårn and get a view of the church nave through the glass panel at the start of the ramp.

8 Universitetet

Founded in 1479 by Christian I, the University of Copenhagen was the country's first university. The Neo-Classical building that can be seen here today dates to the 19th century. In the courtyard, there are the remains of an old Bishop's Palace (1420). Most of the university is now on the island of Amager.

THE BELLS AND CARILLON OF HELLIGÅNDSKIRKEN

In 1647, 50 years after the clock tower was built, king Christian IV gifted the church a set of bells and a carillon. The carillon consisted of 19 bells. It was also used at funerals; the importance of the deceased decided for how long the bells would chime – sometimes hours.

9 Vor Frue Kirke

In the 12th century, Bishop Absalon founded a Gothic church here *(see p39)*. After burning down twice, the present Neo-Classical cathedral **(below)** was completed in 1829, but the tower is from medieval times.

6 Synagogen

Built from 1830–33, Copenhagen's oldest synagogue survived Nazi occupation. The synagogue for the city's Jewish community, it is not open to visitors except with prior booking.

10 Helligåndskirken

The Church of the Holy Ghost *(see p39)* was built in 1295 as a hospital for the weak and elderly, and was expanded to include a monastery in 1474.

NEED TO KNOW
MAP J4

Synagogen: Krystalgade 12; 33 12 88 68

Rundetårn: Købmagergade 52A; 33 73 03 73; open May–Sep: 10am–8pm daily, Oct–Apr: 10am–6pm Mon, Thu–Sun, 10am–9pm Tue–Wed; adm 25 Dkr (free with Copenhagen Card); www.rundetaarn.dk

Trinitatis Kirke: Købmagergade 52A; open 9:30am–4:30pm Mon–Sat; www.trinitatis kirke.dk

Universitetet: Nørregade 10; 35 32 26 26; open 9am–5pm Mon–Fri; www.ku.dk

Vor Frue Kirke: Nørregade 8; open 8am–5pm Mon–Sat

Sankt Petri Kirke: Skt Peders St 2; 33 13 38 33; open Apr–Sep: 11am–3pm Wed–Sat; adm to the sepulchral chapel

Helligåndskirken: Niels Hemmingsens Gade 5; 33 15 41 44; open noon–4pm Mon–Fri (11am–1pm Sat)

Following pages Statue of Frederik V and Marmorkirken, Amalienborg

TOP10 ⭐ Kongens Nytorv and Nyhavn

Kongens Nytorv (King's New Square) and Nyhavn (New Harbour) are two of the most picturesque areas in Copenhagen, although ongoing construction work around Kongens Nytorv has at times marred the view. The square was once outside the city gates and the site of the town gallows in medieval times. The Nyhavn canal was planned by Frederik III to connect the Inner Harbour with the square, enabling merchants to unload their goods.

① Nyhavn Nos 18, 20 and 67

These brightly painted merchants' houses (see p47) were built together with the harbour. Fairy-tale writer Hans Christian Andersen lived in them – he wrote his first tale, *The Tinder Box* (1835), while living at No 20.

③ Nyhavn Canal

Running down to the Inner Harbour, this canal (right) is flanked by houses that belonged to merchants. A large anchor, installed in honour of the sailors who lost their lives in World War II, marks the starting point of Nyhavn.

Kongens Nytorv and Nyhavn

② Charlottenborg Slot

An early example of the Danish Baroque style, this palace was built by Frederik III's son Ulrik. It houses the Royal Danish Academy of Fine Arts as well as the Kunsthal Charlottenborg.

④ Hotel d'Angleterre

This is Copenhagen's oldest hotel (below), and one of the oldest in the world (see p114). It has hosted royalty and celebrities, including Karen Blixen, Churchill, Grace Kelly and Madonna.

⑤ Magasin du Nord

Originally the famous Hotel du Nord, this is Copenhagen's oldest department store and is considered to be the city's answer to London's Selfridges or New York's Bloomingdale's.

⑥ Amber Museum

Set in a house dating back to 1606, this small museum displays an exquisite collection dedicated to Denmark's national gem, amber (also called Nordic Gold).

8 Equestrian Statue

The bronze statue in the middle of Kongens Nytorv commemorates Christian V (1646–99), who rebuilt the square in 1670 in Baroque style. Created by the French-born court sculptor Abraham-César Lamoureux, it shows the king dressed as a Roman emperor **(left)**.

"THE IMPERIAL ETHIOPIAN PALACE"

In the 1950s, Ethopia's emperor Haile Selassie, with his wife, family and entire entourage, visited Denmark and stayed at the Hotel d'Angleterre. During their stay, all telephone calls to the hotel were answered with "The Imperial Ethiopian Palace".

9 Store Strandstræde and Lille Strandstræde

Once full of pubs and brothels, "Big Beach Street" and "Little Beach Street" are now home to art galleries and stylish designer shops.

10 Det Kongelige Teater

This Baroque-style theatre is home to the Royal Danish Ballet **(below)** and is the third one to stand on this site.

7 Vingårdsstræde 6

At the age of 22, Hans Christian Andersen lived for a year in the attic of this building *(see p46)*, one of the city's oldest, built on the site of a vineyard (hence *Vingårdsstræde*). Its 13th-century cellars now host the Michelin-starred Kong Hans Kælder.

NEED TO KNOW

MAP K4–L4

Amber Museum: Kongens Nytorv 2; 33 11 67 00; open May–Sep: 9am–7:30pm daily, Oct–Apr: 10am–5:30pm daily; adm 25 Dkr, child 10 Dkr; www.houseofamber.com

Charlottenborg Slot: Nyhavn 2; 33 74 46 39; open 11am–8pm Tue–Fri, 11am–5pm Sat–Sun; adm 90 Dkr, concessions 40 Dkr, free after 5pm Wed; www.kunsthalcharlottenborg.dk

Magasin du Nord: Kongens Nytorv 13; open 10am–8pm daily; www.magasin.dk

Det Kongelige Teater: Kongens Nytorv; 33 69 69 33; guided tours available, book at the box office or in advance; www.kglteater.dk

■ The restaurants on the south side of Nyhavn are good and usually not as busy as those on the north.

■ Find a quick bite away from the crowds in Nyhavn Pizzeria at 8 Lille Strandstræde.

TOP 10 ⭐ Amalienborg and Frederiksstaden

Built in the 1750s, this stately complex was designed by the royal architect, Nicolai Eigtved. Four Rococo palaces, originally home to four noble families, enclose an octagonal square in Frederiksstaden, an aristocratic area built by Frederik V. Christian VII bought the palaces after the Christiansborg Slot burned down in 1794, and the royal family has lived here ever since. It was named after a palace built on this site by Queen Sophie Amalie in the 17th century.

Christian VII's Palace ①

This palace **(right)** was one of the first to be completed by the time of Eigtved's death in 1754. Also known as Moltke Palace – named after its original owner, Count Adam Gottlob Moltke – it is the most expensive palace in the complex and also boasts one of the best Rococo interiors in the entire country.

③ Frederik VIII's Palace

This palace, which has a clock on its façade, was renamed after Frederik VIII moved in. It is now the residence of Crown Prince Frederik and Crown Princess Mary.

⑤ The Golden Axis

Marmorkirken and Frederiksstaden lie on a short axis called the Golden Axis, which was considered very important when the Opera House was built.

④ Amaliehaven

The Amalie Garden was created in 1983 on the banks of the Harbour, financed by the shipping giant A P Møller and the Christine McKinney Møller Foundation. It has a splendid fountain.

② Palace Guards

When the queen is in residence, the Danish Royal Life Guards **(above)** stand outside the palace, guarding their monarch in two-hour shifts. At noon, guards from Rosenborg Slot take over, marching through the city streets just before noon.

NEED TO KNOW

MAP L3

Marmorkirken: Frederiksgade 4; 33 15 01 44; open 10am–7pm Mon–Thu, noon–5pm Fri–Sun (tower open mid-Jun–Aug: 1–3pm daily, Sep–mid-Jun: 1–3pm Sat & Sun); adm; www.marmorkirken.dk

Amalienborg Museum: 33 12 21 86; open May–mid-Jun: 10am–4pm daily; mid-Jun–mid-Sep: 10am–5pm daily; mid-Sep–Oct: 10am–4pm daily; closed Nov–Apr: Mon; adm 95 Dkr, students 65 Dkr, free with Copenhagen Card; www.dkks.dk

■ Two palaces are closed to the public: Frederik VIII's and Christian IX's.

■ The guards will not respond well to people sitting on palace steps.

THE RUSSIAN CONNECTION

The onion domes of Alexander Nevsky Kirke, the Russian Orthodox Church, are easy to identify. Consecrated in 1883, it was a gift from Tsar Alexander III to mark his marriage to the Danish Princess Marie Dagmar in 1866.

7 Colonnade

Christian VII's royal architect, Caspar Harsdorff, built this Classical-style colonnade in 1794–5. Supported by eight ionic columns, it connects two palaces.

8 Christian IX's Palace

The first royal family to live here was Crown Prince Frederik VI and his wife (1794). Since 1967, it has been home to Queen Margrethe and Prince Consort Henrik.

6 Marmorkirken

Properly called Frederikskirken (see p39), the Marble Church (above) got its name on account of plans to build it with Norwegian marble. Its dome, one of the largest in Europe, has a diameter of 31 m (102 ft).

Amalienborg and Frederiksstaden

9 Christian VIII's Palace

This is where Crown Prince Frederik lived until his marriage to Australian Mary Donaldson. Part of the palace is open all year round as the Amalienborg Museum (above).

10 Equestrian Statue of Frederik V

Designed and cast (1753–71) by French sculptor Jacques Saly, this statue of Frederik V (right) is said to have cost four times as much as Amalienborg itself.

TOP 10 ⭐ SMK – National Gallery of Denmark

The National Gallery is housed in two buildings, one from the 19th century and the other a stylish, modern extension, linked by a bridge over Sculpture Street. The museum holds international and national paintings, sculptures, prints, drawings and installations from the 14th century to the present, with the national collection specializing in Golden Age and 19th-century paintings.

1 The Meeting of Joachim and Anne outside the Golden Gate of Jerusalem

Filippino Lippi (1457–1504) was a true Renaissance artist. This is evident in the architectural detail of the Corinthian columns and his paintings (above).

2 The Wheel of Life

Belonging to the *Suite of Seasons* series, this painting (1953) by Asger Jorn *(see p45)* represents the month of January. Jorn, who was suffering from tuberculosis, was inspired to paint this in the hope of better health.

3 The X-Room

This space has changing installations by young international artists. The black box interior is transformed into multimedia worlds.

4 Please, Keep Quiet!

Visitors have to enter this installation by Elmgreen and Dragset (2003) through swing doors, which open to a hospital ward scene. This represents the neutrality of an exhibition space.

5 Sculpture Street

An impressive, varied collection of sculptures by international contemporary artists runs the length of the building under a glass roof.

6 Christ as the Suffering Redeemer

This striking painting (1495–1500) on the traditional pietà theme by prominent Renaissance artist Andrea Mantegna shows the Resurrection of Christ on the third day after his crucifixion. Mantegna is known for his profound interest in ancient Roman civilization; in this painting it comes through in the porphyry sarcophagus.

7 Alice

One of over 300 portraits by Amedeo Modigliani painted between 1915 and 1920, this beautiful painting, with simple, stylized features, reflects the artist's interest in African sculpture (below).

8 Romantic Paintings

Per Kirkeby is one of Denmark's most important living artists. This early collage from 1965 uses clippings from popular magazines and comics as a homage to Pop Art.

Key to Floorplan
- Ground floor
- First floor
- Second floor

Please, Keep Quiet! 4

The Wheel of Life 2

Artemis 9

Portrait of Madame Matisse 10

The X-Room 3

Alice 7

Romantic Paintings 8

The Meeting of Joachim and Anne outside the Golden Gate of Jerusalem 1

Sculpture Street 5

Christ as the Suffering Redeemer 6

National Gallery Floorplan

9 Artemis

Created in 1893–4, Vilhelm Hammershøi's painting **(above)** shows the goddess Artemis crowned with a crescent moon. The painting's Arcadian nudity, lack of depth, muted palate and enigmatic coolness are typical of Hammershøi's later work.

10 Portrait of Madame Matisse

Also known as *The Green Stripe*, this painting by Henri Matisse of his wife was to have far-reaching repercussions in the art world. It was one of several radical paintings shown in the 1905 *Salon d'Automne* and helped give rise to the Fauvist movement, known for its bright colours and spontaneous style.

NEED TO KNOW

MAP J2 ■ Sølvgade 48–50 ■ www.smk.dk

Open 11am–5pm Tue–Sun (until 8pm Wed)

Adm 110 Dkr; under-30s 85 Dkr; under-18s free

Free guided tours available

■ The prints and drawings collection dates back to the 15th century.

■ The children's museum provides activities every weekend throughout the summer holidays.

■ The bright, stylish museum café looks out onto Østre Anlæg Lake. In good weather, the park is ideal for a picnic.

Museum Guide
Enter the museum from the corner of Sølvgade and Øster Voldgade. The lobby has temporary exhibitions and a bookshop. The entire ground floor is taken up by Sculpture Street, with 20th-century Danish and international art in the extension of the first and second floor. The old main building houses European art 1300–1800, Danish and Nordic art 1750–1900 and French art 1900–1930.

🔟 ⭐ Christiania

A world apart from the opulent splendour of Royal Copenhagen, this self-proclaimed "freetown" sits on the edge of one of the city's most expensive neighbourhoods. It has provided a safe haven for hippies, dreamers and nonconformists since the 1970s, when a band of ideological squatters moved into the abandoned army barracks with the aim of creating a self-sustaining community, free from the shackles of the state. Today, it's a bucolic, tumbledown wonderland of cosy cafés, bars, music venues, art galleries and shops.

Entrance to Christiania and Pusher Street

1 Den Grå Hal
With its graffitied entrance, this is the biggest music and cultural venue in the freetown of Christiania. The former stables doubles up as a unique bazaar during the Christmas period, selling everything – even locally carved instruments.

2 Badehuset
Dare to go bare at this back-to-basics nudist bathhouse; the cheapest and friendliest unisex sauna in the city. For under 50 Dkr, you can try a wonderful Moroccan *rasul* (a mineral cleanser).

3 Christiania Walking Tour
To really get a feel for the area, join one of the regular walking tours of Christiania and learn more about the fascinating history of the self-styled freetown from one of its residents. Tours depart regularly.

4 Nemoland
This former fruit and vegetable market is now one of Copenhagen's most vibrant bars, offering cheap booze and eats to be enjoyed on its terrace (**below**). The outdoor stage hosts regular free music concerts in the summer.

5 ALIS Wonderland

What started life as a humble skate ramp has become one of the city's best skateparks. The vibrant graffiti murals **(above)** adorning the walls are now an attraction in themselves.

8 Café Månefiskeren

This cosy café with a laid-back vibe is the perfect spot to unwind or enjoy a game of bar billiards. There's regular free jazz and reggae concerts in the quaint cobblestone courtyard.

CASTLE ISLAND

In 2004, as residents of Christiania sought to gain permanent rights from the government to occupy the area, they tried to appease the state by tearing down the colourful hash stalls that brazenly lined Pusher Street at the time. One such booth, the interestingly named "Smoke-away" stall, survived intact and has been displayed in the city's Nationalmuseet.

Christiania

10 Loppen

This intimate live music venue **(below)** is a cornerstone of the city's alternative music scene. With gigs almost every night of the week, and a great programme that includes everything from Scandinavian punk to Danish dub-reggae, it's the ideal place to end your night out.

6 Morgenstedet

Tuck into hearty vegetarian fare at this cosy cottage-style restaurant set just off Christiania's main drag. It was first established many years ago as a volunteer-run collective.

9 Christiania Smedie

Christiania's oldest business, this blacksmith started out producing furnaces in the early 1970s before switching its attention to building cargo bikes.

7 Galloperiet

Christiania's tongue-in-cheek tribute to the SMK – National Gallery of Denmark, this quirky gallery has a collection of wonderful arts and crafts.

NEED TO KNOW

MAP M5 ▪ Prinsessegade, ▪ www.christiania.org

▪ Christiania is a car-free community, so it is best not to travel there on four wheels. On-street parking outside the pedestrianized zone is limited, so hop on a bike, or take the 9A bus from the Central Station.

▪ Visitors are advised not to film or photograph in Christiania.

▪ The possession and sale of cannabis are still illegal in Denmark. While police rarely venture into Christiania itself, officers regularly conduct stop-checks on people leaving the commune.

TOP 10 ⭐ Slotsholmen

The small fishing village of Copenhagen was founded on the island of Slotsholmen in the 12th century. Bishop Absalon, the king's friend, built a castle here in 1167. Two centuries later, the castle was destroyed by the Hanseatic League, the European trade alliance, which resented Copenhagen's increasing control over trade. Christiansborg Slot, which stands here today, is home to the Danish Parliament, the Jewish Museum and the Palace Church.

1 Christianborg Tårnet
At 106 m (348 ft), the tower of Christiansborg Slot is the highest in Copenhagen and offers a magnificent panoramic view of the city. It is free to enter (closed Monday), but be sure to reserve in advance if you want to eat in the tower's upscale Nordic restaurant.

2 Christiansborg Slotskirke
On the site of the original 18th-century church destroyed in the ferocious palace fire of 1794, this Neo-Classical church was built in 1813–26 (see p39). However, a fire broke out in 1992 and destroyed its roof, dome and even parts of the interior. The royal family still uses the palace chapel for baptisms as well as when royal family members lie in state.

3 Thorvaldsens Museum
This museum is home to almost all of the works and some of the personal belongings of Danish sculptor Bertel Thorvaldsen (see p45). In the entrance hall (below) are the original plaster casts of his most famous pieces.

4 Danish War Museum
Built as an arsenal in 1604–8, the Royal Danish Arsenal Museum is filled with artillery guns. The Armoury Hall has 7,000 hand weapons, some from the 1300s.

5 Christiansborg Slot
Designed in Neo-Baroque style in 1907–28, this palace is where you will find the Folketinget (the Parliament), the Prime Minister's apartment, the High Court and the State Rooms (above) used for royal family functions – note the marble- and silk-adorned Throne Room and Great Hall.

6 Teatermuseet
This delightful court theatre, above the Royal Stables, was established in 1767. Now a museum (see p44), it depicts Danish theatre in the 18th and 19th centuries. Visitors can also walk onto the stage.

8 Dansk Jødisk Museum

This museum has a striking, modern interior **(left)**, designed by Polish-American architect Daniel Libeskind. The building brilliantly depicts the lives and culture of the Jewish population staying in Denmark *(see p44)*.

9 Ruins Under the Palace

These fascinating ruins were discovered during the construction of the present palace. Notable are parts of Bishop Absalon's castle, the second castle that stood here until the 18th century, and details of the routine of daily life.

CASTLE ISLAND

Several castles have stood on this island through the centuries. The first one was built in 1167 by Bishop Absalon. A second castle, used by King Erik of Pomerania, was built in 1416. When the building started to fall apart, it was pulled down and demolished in 1731 by Christian VI who, in its place, built a palace suitable for an Absolute Monarch. It was completed in 1740, but was destroyed in the fire of 1794. Another castle, built in 1803–28, burned down in 1884. The present castle was built in 1907–28.

10 Royal Library Gardens

With blossoming beds of flowers and large shadowy trees **(below)**, this garden is centered around a fountain *(see p51)*, and there are plenty of benches to sit on and relax, as you look at the statue of philosopher Søren Kierkegaard.

7 Royal Stables

The stables of Christian VI's Palace survived the fire of 1794. The Queen's horses are still kept here amid splendid marble walls, columns and mangers. There is also a collection of royal coaches and riding gear.

NEED TO KNOW

MAP J5

Christiansborg Slot: 33 92 64 92; open May–Sep: 10am–5pm daily, Oct–Apr: 10am–5pm Tue–Sun; tours of State Rooms May–Sep: 3pm daily, Oct–Apr: 3pm Tue–Sun; adm 90 Dkr, under-18s free; www.christiansborg.dk

Ruins Under the Palace: open May–Sep: 10am–5pm daily, Oct–Apr: 10am–5pm Tue–Sun; adm 50 Dkr, under-18s free

Royal Stables: open May–Sep: 1:30–4pm daily, Oct–Apr: 1:30–4pm Tue–Sun; adm 50 Dkr, under-18s free

Royal Library Gardens: 6am–10pm daily

Christiansborg Slotskirke: open 10am–5pm daily

Danish War Museum: 33 11 60 37; open noon–4pm Tue–Sun

Thorvaldsens Museum: Bertel Thorvaldsens Plads 2; 33 32 15 32; open 10am–5pm Tue–Sun; adm 70 Dkr (free Wed), under-18s free; www.thorvaldsensmuseum.dk

TOP 10 ⭐ Nationalmuseet

Denmark's largest museum, the National Museum presents the history and culture of the Danes from prehistoric times through to the present. It also houses a wonderful collection of Greek and Egyptian antiquities, an ethnographic collection and the Children's Museum. Many of the displays derive from King Frederik III's Royal Cabinet of Curiosities, put together around 1650.

NEED TO KNOW

MAP J5 ■ Ny Vestergade 10 ■ 33 13 44 11 ■ www.natmus.dk

Open Jul–Aug: 10am–5pm daily; Sep–Jun: 10am–5pm Tue–Sun

Free guided tours: Jul: 10:30am, noon, 1:30pm daily; Aug–Sep: 10:30am, noon, 1:30pm Sat & Sun; Oct–Dec: 10:30am, 1:30pm Sat & Sun

Victorian Home: Frederiksholms Kanal 18; open 11am–1pm (every hour) Sat & Sun (only via a guided tour, buy tickets at the museum); adm 50 Dkr, under-18s free

■ The Victorian Home, a plush apartment with beautiful, authentic 19th-century interiors, owned by the museum, is located nearby.

■ Have brunch or open sandwiches at the café.

Museum Guide

Fronted by a courtyard, the entrance hall has toilets, lockers and the museum shop, selling books and educational toys with a Viking twist. The Children's Museum (*see p52*) is to your left. The ground floor has the prehistoric collection, while the first floor has a range of displays. There's a Danish history collection on the second floor, and the antiquities are on the third floor. Temporary exhibitions rotate regularly.

1 Room 117

This 18th-century bourgeois interior can be traced to the town of Aalborg in Jutland. A room in a sea of glass-display galleries, it features a heavy wooden four-poster bed **(above)**, chest, coffered wooden ceiling and mullioned windows.

2 Denmark's Oldest Coin

The name of Denmark and an image of a Danish king are depicted on this silver coin, displayed in Room 144, that was struck in AD 995.

5 Gundestrup Cauldron

Found near Gundestrup, this lovely silver cauldron from the Iron Age is decorated with animals and mystical figures.

3 Prehistoric Denmark and the Viking Age

The museum's most popular exhibit is this display of the country's 14,000-year history. These intricate golden horns **(right)** were reconstructed in the 20th century.

4 Cylinder Perspective Table

Part of Frederik III's Royal Cabinet of Curiosities, the table shows him and his wife painted ingeniously in a distorted perspective, rectified when viewed in the reflective cylinder.

Sun Chariot 6

The unique Sun Chariot or Solvognen (right) was dug up in 1902 by a farmer who was ploughing his field. This 3,400-year-old artifact from the Bronze Age shows a wheeled horse pulling a large sun disk gilded on one side.

Nationalmuseet Floorplan

Key to Floorplan
- Ground floor
- First floor
- Second floor
- Third floor

Prehistoric Denmark and the Viking Age — 3

State Rooms — 8

Room 117 — 1

Denmark's Oldest Coin — 2

Gundestrup Cauldron — 5

China, Japan and the Far East — 9

Inuit Culture — 7

Cylinder Perspective Table — 4

Sun Chariot — 6

Oak Burial Coffins — 10

China, Japan and the Far East 9

The Far East is well represented in this marvellous collection that includes Japanese laquerwork, fabulously costumed Samurai warriors, replete with weaponry, and beautiful Imperial Dragon robes.

Oak Burial Coffins 10

Seven Bronze-Age oak coffins (below), dating back to 1,400 BC, occupy the ground floor. The Egtved grave, which holds the body of a fully clad young woman, is an extraordinary exhibit.

Inuit Culture 7

This collection from Greenland showcases the skill and creative ingenuity of the people of the frozen North. The displays include clothing, such as embroidered anoraks and boots, plus toys and watercolours of daily life.

State Rooms 8

The State Rooms date back to the time when this building was a royal palace. They have been well preserved and are virtually intact from the period 1743–4. Next-door, the Great Hall is adorned with the original Flemish tapestries.

The Top 10 of Everything

Marble sculptures at the Ny
Carlsberg Glyptotek museum

🔟 Moments in History

1 **c.1000: Bishop Absalon's Castle**

Copenhagen was founded around AD 1000 on Slotsholmen *(see p30)* and prospered greatly from the shoals of herring that appeared in its waters. In the 1160s Havn was given by Valdemar I to his adviser, Bishop Absalon, who built a castle as protection against raiders. The prosperity of Havn became a threat to the Hanseatic League. They attacked the castle, destroying it in 1369.

Statue of Bishop Absalon

2 **1416: Copenhagen, Capital of Denmark**

King Erik VII (also called Erik of Pomerania) took up residence in the second castle in 1416, by which time Havn was a major economic centre. It was proclaimed the capital of Denmark in 1443.

3 **1479: The Founding of the University of Copenhagen**

King Christian I inaugurated the University of Copenhagen on 1 June 1479. It had four faculties – Theology, Law, Medicine and Philosophy – and

like others of the time was part of the Roman Catholic Church. It was re-established in 1537 by Christian III after the Reformation.

4 **1534–36: Civil War and Reformation**

Between 1534 and 1536, the Protestant Christian III successfully withstood an uprising against him that favoured Christian II, his Catholic cousin. Christian III brought about the Reformation in Denmark.

5 **1657: Wars with Sweden**

The Swedes and Danes were in dispute over the Sound. In 1657, the Swedes crossed the Sound on foot, attacking Copenhagen. The Treaty of Roskilde saw Denmark cede its Swedish territories.

6 **1660: Absolute Monarchy**

Frederik III introduced Absolute Monarchy in 1660, enhancing the powers of the middle classes of Copenhagen. Later, in 1848, it was abolished by Frederik VII.

Painting of Copenhagen in 1660

1728: The Great Fire
In October, within four days, the greatest fire in the history of Copenhagen wiped out almost all of the north of the city. It began early in the morning at Vester Kvarter 146 – now roughly at the top of Strøget. Five churches, the university library and 1,600 houses were destroyed.

 1801 and 1807: The Battles of Copenhagen
Early in the 19th century, the city suffered more lasting damage when the British attacked in 1801, destroying the Danish navy, and again in 1807 to discourage the Danes from supporting France in the Napoleonic Wars.

The Battles of Copenhagen

 1943: Rescue of the Danish Jews
The Nazis occupied Denmark during World War II from 1940 to 1945. In 1943, when they ordered that all Danish Jews were to be deported to Germany, a collective of Danes and Swedes secretly evacuated virtually the entire Jewish population to Sweden by sea. As a result, most Danish Jews survived the war.

1999: The Øresund Bridge
Connecting Copenhagen to Malmö, Sweden, the Øresund Bridge is an impressive piece of architecture. The bridge also has significant symbolic meaning, representing a collaboration between the Swedes and the Danes who were arch enemies in the past.

TOP 10 HISTORICAL FIGURES

A portrait of King Harald Bluetooth

1 Harald Bluetooth (911–987)
King Harald converted the country of Denmark to Christianity.

2 King Cnut (994/5–1035)
Cnut ruled England, Norway and Denmark for 20 years and famously failed to hold back the waves.

3 Bishop Absalon (1128–1201)
Counsellor to King Valdemar I, he built the first castle on Slotsholmen.

4 Tycho Brahe (1546–1601)
Brahe's astronomical tables were used to plot the rules of planetary motion.

5 Christian IV (1577–1648)
Christian IV promoted shipping and overseas trade and built the Rundetårn and Rosenborg Slot.

6 Vitus Jonassen Bering (1681–1741)
A fearless Danish explorer who discovered the Bering Strait, Sea, Island and Land Bridge.

7 Hans Christian Ørsted (1777–1851)
Danish physicist and chemist who discovered electromagnetism.

8 Søren Kierkegaard (1813–55)
A Danish philosopher who first put forward the theory of "existentialism".

9 Knud Rasmussen (1879–1933)
The first man to cross the Northwest Passage by dogsled.

10 Niels Bohr (1885–1962)
A Nobel Prize-winner (1922), Bohr's research contributed vastly to the understanding of quantum mechanics.

🔟 Churches

Gilded Baroque altarpiece inside Holmens Kirke

① Holmens Kirke
Built from 1562–3 as a naval forge, it was converted into a church (see p41) in 1619. The pulpit is the tallest in Denmark, and the Baroque altarpiece is exceptionally ornate.

② Grundtvigs Kirke
På Bjerget 14B, Bispebjerg ▪ 35 81 54 42 ▪ Open 9am–4pm Mon–Sat (to 6pm Thu), noon–4pm Sun (Nov–Apr: to 1pm) ▪ www. grundtvigskirke.dk

This parish church was built by P V Jensen Klint and his son, Kaare Klint, from 1921–6. It has yellow-brick walls and a modern Gothic appearance.

③ Trinitatis Kirke
Standing next door to the Rundetårn is the Trinitatis Kirke (see p19). Commissioned by Christian IV in 1637, this lovely church was completed in the reign of Frederik III in 1656. The present interior dates back to 1731, as the original was burnt in the fire of 1728. It includes boxed pews with seashell carvings, a gilded altarpiece, a Baroque dark wood pulpit and a fabulous gold and silver organ.

④ Christians Kirke
Built in the Rococo style in 1755–9 by Nicolai Eigtved, Frederik V's master architect, Christians Kirke (see p93) is starkly different from most Danish churches. Instead of the congregation sitting only in pews in the nave, the church has a second gallery level (like that of a theatre) where all the important worshippers were seated.

⑤ Vor Frelsers Kirke
This splendid Baroque church (see p94) was built in 1682–96 at the behest of Christian V. The king's royal insignia can be seen at various places in the church, including on the organ

Imposing exterior of Grundtvigs Kirke

case, which is supported by elephants, the symbol of Denmark's prestigious Order of the Elephant *(see p43)*. The spire is 90 m (295 ft) high, and the tower affords a magnificent view of the city. The interior of the church is bright and well lit, thanks to the white walls and tall windows.

6 Helligåndskirken

Dating back to the 12th century, these are among the oldest architectural remains in the city of Copenhagen. Only Helligåndshuset (now used for markets and monthly exhibitions), Christian IV's Baroque portal and Griffenfeld's Chapel survive. Much of the original church *(see p19)* burnt down in the fire of 1728. The church re-opened after reconstruction in 1732.

7 Vor Frue Kirke

Known as St Mary's Cathedral, the church *(see p19)* has been on this site in different forms since the 12th century and has played host to royal and national events over the years. It has a 19th-century façade and a bright interior dominated by statues of Christ and his Apostles.

8 Sankt Petri Kirke

This is the city's oldest church *(see pp18–19)*. Unlike most medieval buildings, it survived the fire of 1728. Its tower, nave and choir date back

to the 15th century, while the north and south transepts were added years later, in 1634.

9 Christiansborg Slotskirke

The original 18th-century Rococo creation *(see pp30–31)* was destroyed in the palace fire of 1794 and was rebuilt in a Neo-Classical style. Inaugurated on Whit Sunday in 1826, it succumbed to another fire in 1992, but has now been rebuilt.

Ornate interior of Marmorkirken

10 Marmorkirken

This church *(see pp24–5)*, designed in the shape of a circle by Nicolai Eigtved in 1740, has an imposing presence. Work on the building was suspended in 1770 because of increasing expenses, and resumed after nearly 150 years. Eventually, it was inaugurated on 19 August 1894.

TOP10 Landmark Buildings

Entrance to the Rundetårn

1 Rundetårn

This curious Round Tower *(see p18)* was built by Christian IV and affords a wonderful view over the city's old town. It also has a popular gallery that holds innovative, changing exhibitions.

2 Den Sorte Diamant

The Black Diamond *(see p64)* was built by architects Schmidt, Hammer and Lassen. It houses the National Museum of Photography, the Queen's Hall concert space, an exhibition area and Søren K, a smart restaurant. The shiny tiled exterior is highly reflective and a favourite photo opportunity for the boat-trippers floating past *(see p12)*.

3 Børsen

MAP K5 ■ Børsgade ■ Closed to the public

The stock exchange is remarkable for its tower with a striking spire design. The three crowns at the top of the building represent Denmark, Sweden and Norway.

4 Rosenborg Slot

This lovely, turreted Renaissance castle *(see pp16–17)* was built by Christian IV. Now a royal museum, its collections and interior provide a vivid picture of the monarchy over the centuries. The crown jewels are in the basement.

5 Regensen

Built by Christian IV in the 17th century as a student hostel, Regensen *(see p18)* still retains that function today. Unfortunately, most of the original building was burnt down in the city fire of 1728, but it was rebuilt shortly after.

6 Christiansborg Slot

This Neo-Baroque palace *(see pp30–31)*, built in the early 20th century, is the seat of the government and the fifth palace to have been built on the site. Visit the ruins of the first two castles, the theatre and stables and the State Rooms.

7 Frederiksborg Slot

This beautiful, grand Renaissance castle *(see p100)* is a short train ride out of the city. Originally built by Christian IV, it now houses The Museum of National History. Don't miss the castle's ornate chapel.

Garden at Frederiksborg Slot

8 Radisson Blu Royal Hotel

Designed by Danish architect Arne Jacobsen, this hotel *(see p116)* underwent a makeover in the 1980s. The original interior was retained only in Room 606; if it is unoccupied you might be able to have a look at it. The foyer has a 1960s retro look and includes Jacobsen's Swan and Egg chairs *(see p88)*. You can enjoy views of the city from the restaurant.

9 Operaen

The Opera House *(see pp94–5)* auditorium is a masterpiece of acoustic design, from the velour seats that don't absorb sound to the distance from the front of the stage to the back wall, which allows for the perfect time to achieve greatest clarity. Over 100,000 pieces of 23.75 carat gold leaf make up the ceiling.

Waterfront Operaen

10 Holmens Kirke

MAP K5 ■ Holmens Kanal ■ 33 13 61 78 ■ Open 10am–4pm Mon, Wed, Fri & Sat, 10am–3:30pm Tue & Thu, noon–4pm Sun

The only Renaissance church in Copenhagen was built as a sailors' forge in 1562–3 and converted into a church by Christian IV in 1619. The metal fence shows golden elephants carrying black castles on their backs, the royal Danish elephant.

TOP 10 STATUES

Visit Carlsberg's Elephant Gate

1 The Elephant Gate
MAP A6
Big, splendid elephants at the Visit Carlsberg gate.

2 Gefionspringvandet
MAP M2
Fountain depicting the goddess Gefion as she drives an animal-led chariot and ploughs Zealand *(see p80)*.

3 Fiskerkone
MAP J4
The *Fishwife* was created in 1940 and installed at this spot.

4 Lurblæserne
MAP H5
It is said that the *Hornblowers* will sound the Viking horns whenever a virgin passes by.

5 Frederik V
MAP L3
Sculptor Jacques Saly took 18 years to finish this statue *(see p25)*. Unveiled in 1771, it merited a 27-gun salute.

6 Christian V
MAP J3
This shows the king dressed as a Roman emperor on horseback *(see p23)*.

7 Hans Christian Andersen
MAP H5
Famous sculpture by Henry Lukow-Nielsen *(see p72)*.

8 Hans Christian Andersen
MAP J2
Includes scenes from his fairy tales.

9 Caritas Springvandet
MAP H4
One of the oldest statues in Copenhagen, dating back to 1608.

10 The Little Mermaid
MAP M1
This is the city's icon, inspired by the famous fairy tale *(see p80)*.

🔟 Sights of Royal Copenhagen

Chandeliers and artworks in the opulent hallway of Christiansborg Slot

① Christiansborg Slot

This is the fifth castle *(see p30)* on this site. The first, Bishop Absalon's fortified castle (1167), was destroyed in 1369. The castle built in 1740 was the first to be called Christiansborg; it was destroyed by fire in 1794. In the present day, the castle is home to the Danish Parliament.

② Fredensborg Slot

Slottet 1B, 3480 Fredensborg ▪ 20 20 10 12 ▪ Bus 173E ▪ Open Jul and first week of Aug: 12:30pm–4pm (with guided tours of palace and gardens); gardens: Jul 9am–5pm ▪ Adm; free entry to gardens

This 18th-century Baroque palace is the summer home of the Queen. The beautiful gardens here are among the largest in Denmark.

③ Kronborg Slot

This castle *(see p104)*, built as a fortress in the 15th century, was used as a prison and army barracks until 1922. It is now occasionally used for royal functions. You may even hear a salute being fired whenever the royal yacht passes by.

④ Frederiksborg Slot

Christian IV built this Dutch Renaissance-style castle *(see p100)* between 1602 and 1620. It is notable for its spires, copper roofs and sweeping gables. After it was destroyed in a fire in 1859, the Carlsberg Brewery magnate J. C. Jacobsen helped rebuild it. The gardens are the only royal gardens to have escaped being updated to the 19th-century Romantic style.

⑤ Amalienborg

Two of the palaces *(see pp24–5)* here are open to the public; the other two are royal homes. Queen Margrethe resides in Christian IX's Palace and Crown Prince Frederik in Frederik VIII's Palace.

Fredensborg Slot

6 Crown Jewels

These symbols *(see p16)* of monarchy, kept in the stronghold basement of Rosenborg Slot, include the crown, sceptre, orb, sword of state, ampulla (flask for anointing the monarch) and royal jewellery.

7 Rosenborg Slot

This delightful Renaissance palace *(see pp16–17)* is the oldest royal palace still standing in its original form. Set in Kongens Have, it also has a delightful rose garden.

8 Royal Copenhagen Porcelain

The traditional Royal Copenhagen design, "Blue Floral", dates back to the factory's *(see p73)* initiation in 1775. The pottery features a blue design because in earlier times cobalt was the only colour able to withstand extremely high firing temperatures.

Pottery at Royal Copenhagen

9 Roskilde Domkirke

Danish royals, including Harald Bluetooth *(see p37)*, have been buried at Roskilde since the 12th century. The cathedral *(see p102)* houses 39 tombs, the oldest belonging to Margrethe I (d.1412) .

10 Vor Frue Kirke

St Mary's Cathedral *(see p19)* has been a place of royal ceremony since the 13th century and was the setting for the marriage of Margrethe I to King Håkon VI of Norway in 1363. The weddings of Christian I (1449) and Crown Prince Frederik (2004) also took place here.

TOP 10 CROWN JEWELS

1 Christian IV's Crown
Made in 1595–6 by Dirich Fyring, this crown features diamonds, gold, enamel and pearls.

2 The Queen's Crown
The large, square, table-cut diamonds in Queen Sophie Magdalene's crown of 1731 are believed to have come from Queen Sophie Amalie's crown (1648).

3 Baptismal Set
Four-piece gold and silver baptismal set (1671), thought to have been first used for Crown Prince Frederik.

4 Regalia
Sceptre, orb, globe and ampulla made for Frederik III's coronation. Used at subsequent coronations until 1840.

5 Order of the Elephant
The order was founded by Christian I around 1460. The chain is made of gold, enamel, diamonds and pearls.

6 Order of the Dannebrog
Established in 1671 as part of the measures introduced by the Absolute monarchs to manage their subjects.

7 Jewellery Sets
Includes pearl set (1840) made from Charlotte Amalie's jewellery; diamond set (18th century); emerald set (1723).

8 Oldenburg Horn
This is an enamelled, silver-gilt drinking horn.

9 The King's Law 1665
Absolutism's constitution, made from parchment, silk, gold and silver.

10 Christian V's Crown
Christian V's Absolutist crown (1670–71) has a large, rare sapphire believed to be a present from the Duke of Milan to Christian I in 1474.

The stunning crown of Christian V

🔟 Museums and Galleries

The Danish Jødisk Museum

1 Dansk Jødisk Museum

MAP K5 ■ Proviant-passangen 6 ■ 33 11 22 18 ■ Open Sep–May: 1pm–4pm Tue–Fri, noon–5pm Sat–Sun; Jun–Aug: 10am–5pm Tue–Sun ■ Adm; free with Copenhagen Card ■ www.jewmus.dk

The Danish Jewish Museum tells the story of Denmark's Jewish community. Designed by architect Daniel Libeskind, the interlocking interior symbolizes Danish–Jewish good relations, its apogee the rescue of 7,000 Jews from the Nazis.

2 Designmuseum Danmark

Denmark's largest museum *(see p79)* devoted to design, the Designmuseum holds Chinese and Japanese artifacts, along with European medieval and Rococo arts. The other half is dedicated to cutting-edge Danish 20th- and 21st-century design.

The Ny Carlsberg Glyptotek

3 Teatermuseet

MAP J5 ■ Christiansborg Ridebane 18 ■ 33 11 51 76 ■ Open noon–4pm Tue–Sun ■ Adm; free with Copenhagen Card ■ www.teatermuseet.dk

On display at this enthralling museum are sections including the stage, the auditorium and dressing rooms of the 18th-century Royal Theatre *(see p46)* that survived the devastating fire of 1794.

4 Frihedsmuseet

The Museum of Danish Resistance *(see p79)* explores Danish life during the Nazi occupation of 1940–45. The museum is currently closed until the end of 2019 due to extensive fire damage.

5 Nationalmuseet

At Denmark's largest museum of cultural history *(see pp32–3)* you can explore the history of the Danes right up to the present day. Artifacts range from Iron Age burials and Renaissance interiors to African masks and houses on stilts. Check out the museum's spectacular ethnographic collection, including the world's oldest painting by South American Indians.

6 Ny Carlsberg Glyptotek

This museum *(see p70)* houses a fabulous collection of antiquities from the Mediterranean coast, Egypt, Greece and Rome. You will also find an impressive collection of 19th- and 20th-century Danish and French fine art on display.

7 Cisternerne – The Cisterns

Beneath the manicured lawns of Frederiksberg Have, this exhibition space (see p88) is remarkable for both its provocative contemporary art and film installations and the singularity of its setting: a 19th-century cistern.

8 Davids Samling

Set inside a 19th-century town house, the museum (see p78) holds the collections of Christian Ludvig David (1878–1960), a Danish barrister. It includes some fabulous furniture as well as ancient Islamic ornamental art.

The entrance of SMK

9 SMK – National Gallery of Denmark

Nestled in a park with lakes and grassy slopes, the SMK (see pp26–7) displays a collection of international art, with works by Great Masters like Dürer and Titian and by icons such as Picasso and Matisse. These are displayed with 20th-century Danish works, including those of the CoBrA group.

10 Thorvaldsens Museum

Opened in 1848, this museum (see pp32–3) pays homage to the Neo-Classical sculptor Bertel Thorvaldsen. It includes most of his works, as well as some private belongings. You can also visit his grave.

TOP 10 DANISH ARTISTS

Sculpture by Bertel Thorvaldsen

1 Bertel Thorvaldsen (1770–1844)
Son of an Icelandic wood carver, Thorvaldsen became Denmark's most famous sculptor.

2 Christoffer Eckersberg (1783–1853)
Laid the foundations for Denmark's Golden Age of painting (1800–50).

3 Michael Ancher (1849–1927)
One of the best-known artists in Denmark and the unofficial head of the Skagen group.

4 Peder Severin Krøyer (1851–1909)
His work is inspired by the lives of the fishermen of Skagen.

5 Anna Ancher (1859–1935)
A Skagen artist and wife of Michael Ancher. Her work is typified by picturesque scenes of family life.

6 Vilhelm Hammershøi (1864–1916)
Known for his paintings of interiors, done in muted colours.

7 Richard Mortensen (1910–1993)
The first Danish artist to turn to abstraction. Also known for his perfect technical finish.

8 Asger Jorn (1914–73)
Founder of CoBrA, an important art group to emerge after World War II.

9 Bjørn Nørgaard (1947–)
One of the most influential Danish contemporary artists, his works span a range of fields, including sculpture. He also designed the Queen's Tapestries.

10 Olafur Eliasson (1967–)
Danish–Icelandic artist who erects fascinating kinetic sculptures inspired by natural phenomena in cities around the world.

🔟 Hans Christian Andersen Sights

Hotel d'Angleterre, overlooking gardens

1 Hotel d'Angleterre

Hans Christian Andersen lived here (see p114) in November 1860, when he occupied two rooms at the corner of Kongens Nytorv and Østergade (Strøget), close to the Royal Theatre. He also stayed between August 1869 and March 1870, and, finally, during April and May 1871.

2 Det Kongelige Teater

Andersen arrived in the city on 6 September 1819 as a starstruck 14-year-old boy. It was "my second birthday", he recounts in his 1855 biography, The Fairy Tale of My Life. Determined to become an actor, he went straight to the Royal Theatre (see p23) in search of a job. Although he was occasionally employed as an actor, his acting talent never quite matched his skill as a writer.

3 Lille Kongensgade 1
MAP K4

On 23 October 1866, Andersen took a suite of rooms on the third floor here, rented to him by a photographer, Thora Hallager. It was here that he bought furniture for the first time in his life (at the age of 61), as the apartment was an unfurnished one.

4 Rundetårn

The exhibition space (see pp18–19) was once the university library where Andersen spent many hours. His first fairy tale, The Tinderbox (1835), tale of a dog with eyes "as big as a tower" guarding a treasure. Scholars believe this refers to the Rundetårn, which was originally built as an observatory – a literal eye to the sky.

5 Vingårdsstræde 6
MAP K4

Andersen lived here (then No 13) for a year in 1827 in a spartan garret room, preparing for his university exams. This is where he wrote the poem The Student. Once a museum, the room is no longer open to visitors.

6 Bakkehuset

The Bakkehuset (House on the Hill) (see p89) was the home of prominent literary patron Knud L Rahbek and his wife, Kamma, from 1802 to 1830. Andersen met the couple in the early 1820s and their home soon became a meeting place for poets and authors.

Bookshelves in Bakkehuset

⑦ Nyhavn Nos 18, 20 and 67

Andersen lived in lodgings on and around Nyhavn *(see p22)* for much of his life, including at Nyhavn 280 (now No 20) in 1834, No 67 in 1848 and No 18 (a private hotel) in 1871. He lived here until 1875, when he fell terminally ill and moved in with the Melchiors, who then nursed him in their own home.

⑧ Assistens Kirkegård

This is the cemetery *(see p77)* where Andersen's body was interred in Nørrebro. The stone is inscribed with inspirational lines from his poem *Oldingen*, also known as *The Old Man* (1874).

Assistens Kirkegård

⑨ Magasin du Nord

In 1838, Andersen moved into Hotel du Nord, now the department store Magasin du Nord *(see pp22–3)*. Here he proceeded to rent two rooms in the attic, one of which overlooked the Royal Theatre. The next-door Mini's Café became a regular haunt for the writer.

⑩ Vor Frue Kirke

Andersen died on 4 August 1875 of liver cancer. His funeral, a national event attended by the king and crown prince, was held at Vor Frue Kirke *(see p19)* in the old town.

TOP 10 DANISH CULTURAL FIGURES

Actor Viggo Mortensen

1 August Bournonville (1805–1879)
Choreographer and ballet master who created many works.

2 Carl Nielsen (1865–1931)
Composer, violinist and pianist. Best known for his symphonies and the operas *Saul og David* and *Maskerade*.

3 Karen Blixen (1885–1962)
Her famous novel, *Out of Africa* (1937), was published under the pen name Isak Dinesen.

4 Poul Henningsen (1894–1967)
This anti-traditionalist, architect and author is best known for his PH lamps *(see p63)*.

5 Arne Jacobsen (1902–1971)
Architect and designer who defined the concept of Danish design – fluid and practical.

6 Lars von Trier (1956–)
Film director famous for the Dogme95 Collective and his technique of cinematic minimalism.

7 Viggo Mortensen (1958–)
Popular as Aragorn in *The Lord of the Rings* films.

8 Mads Mikkelsen (1965–)
Made his international acting breakthrough as Bond villain Le Chiffre in *Casino Royale*.

9 Helena Christensen (1968–)
Miss Denmark (1986) and a supermodel of the 1990s.

10 Sofie Gråbøl (1968–)
Played detective Sarah Lund in hit crime series *Forbrydelsen (The Killing)*.

⭐10 Outdoor Activities

Browsing the flea market at Nørrebro

1 Flea Markets
Frederiksberg Rådhusplads: MAP A5; Apr–Oct: 8am–3pm Sat ▪ Bertel Thorvaldsens Plads: MAP J5; May–Sep: 8am–5pm Fri, 9am–5pm Sat ▪ Ravnsborggade, Nørrebro: MAP D3; Mar–Nov: 10am–4pm Sun

There are many outdoor flea markets in the summer, offering everything from furniture to vinyl.

2 CopenHot
Refshalevej 325 ▪ 31 32 78 08 ▪ www.copenhot.com

The purveyors of Copenhagen's only floating hot-tub experience, this open-air spa brings Nordic wellness to the city centre. With three giant hot tubs, a sauna with panoramic views of the harbour and five "sailing spa" boats, it's the perfect place to escape the hustle and bustle of the city. There's even speakers to play your own music.

3 Bikes
Almost every major road in Copenhagen has a cycle lane and you can hire a bike (see p109) or use a free City Bike for a day or more.

4 Go Boats
Islands Brygge 10 ▪ 40 26 10 25 ▪ en.goboat.dk

If you prefer to explore the city's waterways at your own pace, hop on board a solar-powered Go Boat and spend an afternoon chugging through the canals. You can buy a picnic hamper or champagne to take on board, although the captain must always remain sober while in control of their vessel!

5 Lounging by the Lakes
Man-made lakes divide the main city from Nørrebro and Østerbro. Of these, Skt Jørgens Sø, Peblinge Sø and Sortedams Sø are easily accessible. You can lounge along their grassy banks or enjoy the scenic view from the bridges.

6 Kongens Have
Attached to Rosenborg Slot, the King's Garden (see p17) is a great place to sunbathe, play frisbee, cricket or football, or have a picnic. In the summer, you can catch a puppet show or a jazz concert.

7 Canal tours
Harbour and canal tours are a lovely way to see the city. There are two canal tour companies (see p13).

Canal tour in Nyhavn

8 Assistens Kirkegård

This beautiful, meandering churchyard (see p77) holds the graves of famous Danes like Hans Christian Andersen, August Bournonville and Niels Bohr.

9 Dyrehaven

MAP B2 ■ Dyrehaven, Klampenborg ■ www.bakken.dk

This deer park has been here since the 16th century and is home to over 2,000 deer (the rutting season is in the autumn). It is like an English park or common and features a noisy, enjoyable funfair, which is called Bakken (see p52).

Elephants at Zoologisk Have

10 Zoologisk Have

You will find polar bears, lions, tigers, elephants and other animals in this delightful zoo (see p88). There are wonderful thematic adventure trails (see p53) for kids.

TOP 10 BEACHES AND POOLS

Diving at Havnebadet

1 Havnebadet
Floating harbour pool (see p64) with fresh water.

2 Bellevue
MAP B2 ■ Strandvejen 340, 2930 Klampenborg
Full of people playing, sailing or relaxing. Left end is nudist.

3 Fælledparkens Soppesø
MAP D2 ■ Borgmester Jensens Allé 50, Østerbro ■ 33 66 36 60
Huge, child-friendly, outdoor pool.

4 Amager Strandpark
MAP B3 ■ Amager Strandvej
Luxury Beach with lagoon, artificial island and snack kiosks.

5 Køge Bugt Strandpark
MAP B3 ■ Ishøj Store Torv 20, 2635 Ishøj
A 7-km (4-mile) beach along Køge Bay.

6 Bellahøj Svømmestadion
MAP B3 ■ Bellahøjvej 1–3, Brønshøj ■ 38 26 21 40
Indoor and outdoor swimming facilities, including water slides.

7 Frederiksdal Friluftsbad
MAP B2 ■ Frederiksdal Badesti 1, Virum ■ 45 83 81 85
Gorgeous lakeside beach with café.

8 DGI-Byen
MAP D5 ■ Corner of Tietgensgade & Ingerslevsgade ■ 33 29 81 40
Indoor facilities with a kids' pool.

9 Charlottenlund Beach
MAP B2 ■ Park Strandvejen 144, Charlottenlund
Good place for sunbathing.

10 Copencabana Havnebadet ved Fisketorvet
MAP E6 ■ Kalvebod Brygge 55, Vesterbro ■ 30 89 04 70
A floating harbour pool.

TOP 10 Off the Beaten Track

Crowds wait outside Mikkeller

1 Mikkeller Baghaven
MAP F3 ■ Refshalevej 169B
■ Opening hours vary; call to confirm

A cavernous bar, taproom and concert venue that specializes in barrel-aged beers, this forms part of the burgeoning beer empire of Mikkel Borg Bjergsø. Offering panoramic views of Copenhagen harbour and regular street-food events, this is the perfect place to while away a sunny afternoon.

2 GoMonkey
MAP B2 ■ Vandtårnsvej 55, Søborg ■ 25 53 30 22 ■ Open 10am–6pm daily

Channel your inner Tarzan at this suburban climbing park in Søborg, which is a 15-minute train ride from central Copenhagen. There are ziplines, rope bridges, high-wires, as well as swing ropes.

3 Meyers Madhus
MAP C3 ■ Nørrebrogade 52 C
■ 35 36 38 37 ■ Open 9am–4pm Mon–Fri

If you'd like to learn how to cook New Nordic, get schooled by the master himself at one of celebrity chef and restaurateur Claus Meyer's Nørrebro cookery classes. Large groups are welcome, but early booking is advised.

4 Amager Strand Beach Park
MAP C3 ■ Amager Strand Promenaden 1 ■ 26 30 24 82 ■ Open May–Sep

Boasting 2.9 miles (4.6 km) of beaches, a world-class skatepark and an open-air concert venue, this sprawling public beach park springs into life in May / June when sun-starved city-dwellers flock to the coast at the first sign of summer.

5 Dragør Havn
MAP C3 ■ Dragør, south of Copenhagen Airport

It may be less than 7 miles (12 km) from central Copenhagen, but this charming fishing village and marina is a world away from the hustle and bustle of the city centre. The settlement dates back to the 12th century, and today still boasts a clutch of immaculately preserved medieval buildings in the traditional Danish style. In the evening, head down to the marina for excellent seafood at local restaurants.

Sailboats at Dragør marina

6 Noma "village"
Refshalevej 96 ■ 32 96 32 97 ■ Open 5pm–midnight Tue–Sat ■ www.noma.dk

An old mining depot situated on Refshaleøen – the next urban island to grow into a destination dining spot – has been beautifully preserved and serves as a new home for Noma, the world-famous restaurant (see p97). The concept is a gastronomic village with different huts for different categories of food preparation, along with an urban farm.

7 Nordic Noir Tours
MAP D5 ■ Vesterport Station ■ nordicnoirtours.com

Discover the darker side of the city with a guided tour of the film locations used in hit crime dramas Forbrydelsen (The Killing), Borgen and The Bridge. Take a peek behind the scenes at each series, and venture into some of the city's lesser-known spots. Tours start from Vesterport Station, and discounts are often offered on pre-bookings.

8 ExitGames
MAP L2 ■ Fredericiagade 30 ■ 71 54 50 05 ■ exitgamescph.dk

Put your sleuthing skills to the test at Copenhagen's premier live escape game, where you must find the hidden objects, figure out the clues and solve the puzzles to earn your freedom and escape from one of three film-themed rooms.

9 Royal Library Gardens
MAP K5 ■ Proviantpassagen 1 ■ Open 6am–10pm daily

Tucked away behind Christiansborg Palace on Slotsholmen island, this secluded public park was built in 1920 on the site of King Christian IV's former naval port. The fountain in the central pool cascades every hour in a nod to the garden's fascinating maritime heritage.

Sunbathing at Royal Library Gardens

10 Frederiksberg Have
Set against the dramatic backdrop of Frederiksberg Slot, this stunning romantic garden (see p87) is an oasis of calm. Between 1798 and 1802 the gardens were landscaped to reflect a typical English garden. Explore its lawns and canals and you might even be rewarded with a glimpse of the elephants at Zoologisk Have (see p88).

🔟 Children's Attractions

Fun for the entire family on board the train at Tivoli

1 Tivoli

The best time to take kids to Tivoli *(see pp14–15)* is during the day, when the atmosphere is more family-oriented. The park's many fun rides include cars on tracks, dragon boats on the lake, the pantomime theatre and the trolley bus.

2 Guinness World Records Museum

This highly popular attraction *(see p72)* brings the Guinness World Records to life. From the utterly bizarre, such as bicycle-eating men, to the internationally renowned in sport and

Guinness World Records Museum

science, 13 galleries celebrate numerous examples of strangeness, ingenuity and determination.

3 World of H C Andersen Museum

Explore the life of Hans Christian Andersen at this charming museum *(see p72)*. It is aimed at kids, who will enjoy the tableaux and recordings of some of his fairy tales. The manuscript of *The Stone and the Wise Man* (1858) may interest bibliophiles.

4 Nationalmuseet

Copenhagen's National Museum *(see pp32–3)* includes an interesting Children's Museum where children are encouraged to participate in a range of activities, including dressing up in grandma's clothes to see how different they are from today's garments, or sitting in an old Danish classroom learning about medieval castles.

5 Bakken

MAP B2 ▪ Dyrehavevej 62 ▪ 39 63 35 44 ▪ www.bakken.dk

If you go down to the woods, you'll find the world's oldest amusement park. Established in 1583, Bakken is a real one-off: a quirky mix of modern thrill rides and vintage sideshows that offers free entry all year round.

6 Experimentarium
MAP B2 ■ Tuborg Havnevej, Hellerup ■ 39 27 33 33 ■ Open 9:30am–5pm Mon–Fri (until 8pm Thu), 10am–5pm Sat–Sun ■ Adm; under-2s free ■ www.experimentarium.dk

This innovative science centre brings science to life via hands-on exploration. Most exhibits are interactive, allowing kids to perform over 300 experiments, and adults can have just as much fun as the kids too. Environmental issues are high on the agenda.

7 SMK – National Gallery of Denmark
The Children's Art Museum at the SMK (see pp26–7) caters to children aged between 4 and 12, with workshops where kids can draw, paint and sculpt; the museum also has a sketching room. On the first Sunday of each month, the museum holds a family day, which includes guided museum tours.

8 Zoologisk Have
This zoo (see p88) is Denmark's largest cultural institution, attracting around 1.2 million visitors every year. Besides the tigers, polar bears and elephants, there are thematic adventure trails and a children's petting zoo. In spring, there tend to be many new baby animals.

9 Den Blå Planet
Denmark's national aquarium (see p100) is the largest in Northern Europe, with over 20,000 marine life forms and seven million litres of water. The aquarium's architecture is certainly worthy of as much attention as its exhibits.

Marine life at Den Blå Planet

10 Fælledparken
Copenhagen's largest public park (see p80), in Østerbro next to the Danish National Stadium, has a fantastic playground featuring multiple tiny trampolines and castles. There is also a skatepark, cafés, sports fields and numerous green lawns for other activities. The park was created between 1906 and 1914 by landscape architect Edvard Glæsel.

Performing Arts and Music Venues

Tables at Wallmans Cirkusbygningen

1 Wallmans Cirkusbygningen

MAP G5 ▪ **Jernbanegade 8** ▪ **33 16 37 00** ▪ **www.wallmans.dk**

Built in 1884, this circular venue was previously a circus building. Today it is used as a glamorous setting for old-fashioned "dinner, show and dancing" evenings. The spectacular entertainment surrounds guests across seven stages while resting members of the cast serve dinner. After the show, it turns into a club.

2 Det Kongelige Teater

World-class performances of ballet are held in Kongens Nytorv *(see p23)*, while dramatic works are performed at the playhouse on the waterfront, Skuespilhuset.

Performance at Det Kongelige Teater

3 Operaen

Famed for its acoustics, the Opera House *(see pp94–5)* attracts a variety of international productions. You can enjoy a good view of the stage from any seat and all the seats are relatively cheap due to government subsidy.

4 Tivoli Concert Hall

The Tivoli Concert Hall *(see pp14–15)* is Copenhagen's largest music venue, with a capacity of 1,900. It stages over 100 operas, ballets and rock and jazz concerts during the Tivoli season.

5 Alice

MAP J4 ▪ **Niels Hemmingsens Gade 10** ▪ **33 15 37 00** ▪ **www.alicecph.com**

Copenhagen's biggest venue for jazz, Alice offers a unique, varied programme. On weekends, late-night concerts kick off at 11pm.

6 Mojo Bluesbar

MAP H5 ▪ **Løngangstræde 21C** ▪ **33 11 64 53** ▪ **www.mojo.dk**

Smoky, small and intimate, this bar is known for its laid-back blues and live jazz performances. There won't be any distracting gimmicks here.

7 Det Ny Teater

MAP C5 ■ Gammel Kongevej 29 ■ 33 25 50 75 ■ www.detny teater.dk

This early 20th-century theatre hosts a variety of popular international musicals, such as *Phantom of the Opera* and *Les Misérables*.

8 Koncerthuset

MAP B3 ■ Ørestads Boulevard 13 ■ 35 20 62 62 ■ www.dr.dk/ koncerthuset

The concert house of the national broadcaster Danmarks Radio (DR) was designed by Jean Nouvel. This landmark building with its blue glass façade has superior acoustics.

Koncerthuset's curved interior

9 Parken

MAP D2 ■ Per Henrik Lings Allé 2 ■ 35 43 31 31 ■ www.teliaparken.dk

This football stadium held its first concert in 2001 with the Eurovision Song Contest. Bands including U2 and Metallica have since performed.

10 VEGA

MAP B6 ■ Enghavevej 40 ■ 33 25 70 11 ■ Club nights: 11pm–4am Fri and Sat; adm: 60 Dkr after 1am ■ www.vega.dk

Occupying a 1950s trade union building, VEGA offers club nights that attract international acts and DJs.

TOP 10 JAZZ VENUES AND EVENTS

Copenhagen Jazz Festival

1 Copenhagen Jazz Festival/ Winter Jazz
In February and July Copenhagen hosts Scandinavia's biggest jazz festival:

2 Charlie Scott's
MAP H4 ■ Skindergade 43 ■ 33 12 12 20
Tiny city-centre bar for jazz lovers.

3 Jazzhus Montmartre
MAP K3 ■ Store Renegade 19a ■ 31 72 34 94
This legendary venue seats 70 people.

4 La Fontaine
MAP J5 ■ Kompagnistræde 11 ■ 33 11 60 98
Known for late sessions Fri and Sat.

5 Huset-KBH
MAP J5 ■ Rådhusstræde 13 ■ 21 51 21 51
Culture house hosts a jazz club.

6 Jazzcup
MAP J3 ■ Gothersgade 107 ■ 33 33 87 40
Both a record store and a café hosting jazz sessions on weekends.

7 Sofie Kælderen
MAP L6 ■ Overgaden Oven Vandet 32 ■ 32 57 77 01
A cornerstone of Copenhagen's jazz scene, attracting big names in jazz.

8 Tango y Vinos
MAP L4 ■ Herluf Trolles Gade 9 ■ 33 32 81 16
Tiny Argentinian wine bar hosting jazz, flamenco, funk and tango musicians.

9 Kind of Blue
MAP D3 ■ Ravnsborggade 17 ■ 26 35 10 56
A small, cozy bar on a hip street.

10 Palæ Bar
MAP K4 ■ Ny Adelgade 5 ■ 33 12 54 71
A favourite hangout for musicians.

TOP 10 Nightlife Venues

Plush, subterranean interior of Copenhagen speakeasy The Jane

1 The Jane
MAP J4 ■ Gråbrødretorv 8 ■ 32 20 75 42 ■ Open 8pm–5am Thu–Sat ■ www.thejane.dk

A night at this part wood-panelled speakeasy, part industrial nightclub is whatever you want it to be. Chat over classic cocktails and soft jazz in the library bar, or cut loose on the hidden dance floor, neatly accessed via a false bookcase.

2 Hive
MAP H4 ■ Skindergade 45–7 ■ 28 45 74 67 ■ Open 11pm–6am Fri and Sat ■ www.hivecph.dk

The city's old courthouse is now a modern nightclub complete with iPhone chargers at the tables.

3 Rust
Trendy Rust (see p82) is at the cutting edge of the local music and clubbing scene. It showcases up-and-coming acts, live music sets and top international DJs.

4 Brass Monkey
MAP B6 ■ Enghavevej 31 ■ Open 8pm–1am Thu, 8pm–4am Fri and Sat ■ www.brassmonkey.dk

Swap the stresses of city life for plastic paradise at Copenhagen's Tiki bar, a kitsch wonderland of exotic cocktails, grass skirts and hula girls.

5 KB3
MAP C6 ■ Kødboderne 3 ■ 33 23 45 97 ■ Open 11pm–late Thu–Sat ■ www.kb3.dk

Housed in a former abattoir, this superclub provides the soundtrack to the meatpacking district's weekend nightlife. The club's backyard is used for open-air parties in the summer.

6 Bakken
MAP C6 ■ Flæsketorvet 19–21 ■ Open 10pm–5am Thu, 8pm–5am Fri and Sat ■ www.bakkenkbh.dk

Not to be confused with the children's theme park in Dyrehaven, this dark, dingy and achingly hip club is a cornerstone of Copenhagen's under-ground music scene.

Revellers at Bakken

7 **Ideal Bar**

MAP B6 ▪ Enghavevej 40
▪ 33 26 09 51 ▪ Open 8pm–1am
selected Weds, 9pm–2am Thu, 10pm–
5am Fri and Sat ▪ idealbar.vega.dk

On the ground floor of trendy venue
VEGA *(see p55)*, this lounge bar offers
club nights with a local vibe. It is
an inexpensive midweek option.

8 **Culture Box**

MAP K2 ▪ Kronprinsessegade
54 ▪ 33 32 50 50 ▪ Open 11pm–6am
Fri and Sat (Culture Box Bar open
from 6pm) ▪ Closed Jun–Jul ▪ Min
age 18 ▪ www.culture-box.com

This purist techno club is one of
Copenhagen's leading venues for
electronic music. Its cocktail bar
opens earlier than the club and
makes a good meeting place.

DJ at work, Culture Box

9 **Hornsleth**

MAP J4 ▪ Lovstraede 4
▪ Open 10pm–5am Fri and Sat
▪ www.hornslethbar.dk ▪ Min age 23

Not for the prudish, this decadent
superclub is a shrine to provocative
Danish artist Kristian von Hornsleth.
The music, however, is less daring,
with DJs spinning a reliable mix
of club classics.

10 **Gefährlich**

Located in the heart of
Nørrebro, known for its club culture,
Gefährlich *(see p82)* (German for
"dangerous") has a restaurant, bar,
art gallery, coffee shop, boutique and
record store. Its nightclub caters to
the tastes of the young and hip.

TOP 10 MICROBREWERIES

The beer menu at Warpigs

1 Warpigs
MAP C6 ▪ Flaesketorvet 25 ▪ 43
48 48 48 ▪ www.warpigs.dk
Brewed on site, with 20 taps daily.

2 Nørrebro Bryghus
MAP D3 ▪ Ryesgade 3, Nørrebro ▪ 35
30 05 30 ▪ www.noerrebrobryghus.dk
Tour this brewery and taste some beer.

3 Vesterbro Bryghus
MAP H5 ▪ Vesterbrogade 2B ▪ 33 11
17 05 ▪ www.vesterbrobryghus.dk
Six Austrian recipe beer brews.

4 BRUS
MAP C3 ▪ Guldbergsgade 29 ▪ 75
22 22 00 ▪ www.tapperietbrus.dk
With 33 beers on tap and an on-site
restaurant, this slick brewpub has it all.

5 Brewpub
MAP H5 ▪ Vestergade 29 ▪ 33 32 00
60 ▪ Closed Sun ▪ www.brewpub.dk
Includes a 17th-century beer garden.

6 Bryggeriet Apollo
MAP G5 ▪ Vesterbrogade 3 ▪ 33
12 33 13 ▪ www.bryggeriet.dk
The original local microbrewery.

7 Ølsnedkeren
MAP C4 ▪ Griffenfeldsgade 52
▪ 22 55 28 70 ▪ www.olsnedkeren.dk
Everything here is made on site.

8 Amager
MAP C5 ▪ Fuglebækvej 2C ▪ 32 50
62 00 ▪ www.amagerbryghus.dk
Tours Mon–Sat by appointment.

9 Mikkeller
Viktoriagade 8, Vesterbro ▪ 33 31
04 15 ▪ www.mikkeller.dk
Set up in 2006, this has its own pub.

10 Kølsters Tolv Haner
MAP C3 ▪ Rantzausgade 56
▪ 32 20 94 84
This place serves its own ecological
beer and cider.

TOP 10 Gay and Lesbian Venues

1 Centralhjørnet
MAP H4 ▪ Kattesundet 18
▪ 33 11 85 49 ▪ Open noon–5am
Sun–Thu, noon–5am Fri & Sat
▪ www.centralhjornet.dk

This is Copenhagen's oldest gay bar, dating from 1852. It holds drag nights; regular shows take place on Thursdays. Kylie Minogue and Europop are jukebox favourites. Sunday afternoons are usually packed with people dancing.

2 Jailhouse
MAP H4 ▪ Studiestræde 12
▪ 33 15 22 55 ▪ Open 3pm–2am Sun–Thu, 3pm–5am Fri & Sat; Restaurant: 6–9pm Thu–Fri ▪ www.jailhouse cph.dk

Kitted out as a prison, this café and event bar has booths like prison cells and staff dressed as prison guards or police officers. There is a restaurant on the second floor; the atmosphere here is relaxed.

3 Oscar Bar and Café
MAP H5 ▪ Regnbuepladsen 7
▪ 33 12 09 99 ▪ Open 10am–midnight Sun–Thu, 10am–2am Fri–Sat (kitchen until 4pm daily) ▪ www.oscarbarcafe.dk

A cosy evening bar and café for the style-conscious, with a long bar and posh leather furniture. The DJ plays funky disco and soulful deep house at the weekends.

Seating at Oscar Bar and Café

Drinks at Masken Bar & Café

4 Masken Bar & Café
MAP H4 ▪ Studiestræde 33
▪ 33 91 09 37 ▪ Open 2pm–3am Sun–Thu, 2pm–5am Fri and Sat
▪ www.maskenbar.dk

One of the oldest LGBT+ bars, Masken hosts live music and drag shows.

5 Café Intime
MAP B5 ▪ Allégade 25, 2000 Frederiksberg ▪ 38 34 19 58 ▪ Open 6pm–2am daily ▪ www.cafeintime.dk

Founded in 1913, this kitsch bar has a predominantly gay crowd. A pianist plays popular classics; you can also enjoy jazz on Sundays.

6 G-A-Y Copenhagen
MAP H4 ▪ Vester Voldgade 10
▪ 33 14 13 30 ▪ Open 6pm–2am Thu, 8pm–5am Fri–Sat

Highly recommended gay night club with drag shows. Music here focuses on pop hits and mainstream tracks.

7 Mens Bar

MAP H4 ■ Teglgårdsstræde 3
■ 33 12 73 03 ■ Open 3pm–2am daily
■ www.mensbar.dk

This strictly all-male, no-frills bar is filled with leather, fascinating tattoos and a dash of denim. Try to catch the free Danish brunch at 3pm on the first Sunday of the month.

8 Never Mind Bar

MAP G4 ■ Nørre Voldgade
■ Open 10pm–6am daily ■ www.nevermindbar.dk

The party rarely stops here at this popular, central LGBT nightclub. If the party is still rocking at 6am, the bartenders will keep the alcohol flowing. There are several dance floors where you can show off your moves. No dress code.

9 Cosy Bar

MAP H4 ■ Studiestræde 24
■ 33 12 74 27 ■ Open 10pm–6am daily ■ www.cosybar.dk

One of Copenhagen's oldest gay bars, Cosy has a small dancefloor. This hangout is often packed with a young crowd and is best visited after 1am.

10 Vela

MAP C5 ■ Viktoriagade 2–4
■ 33 31 34 19 ■ Open 9pm–2am Thu, 9pm–5am Fri and Sat ■ www.vela-gayclub.dk

Attracting a mixed crowd, Vela is a popular lesbian bar with oriental decor in the Vesterbro area. There's table football, small booths and a selection of cheap beers.

TOP 10 GAY AND LESBIAN FESTIVALS AND EVENTS

Copenhagen Pride Festival

1 Torchlight Procession
Last Sun in May ■ www.aidsfondet.dk
This event in memory of people who have died of AIDS takes place on the last Sunday in May.

2 Gaystortion at Distortion
End May–June
Five day techno music festival that takes place on the streets of Copenhagen.

3 St Hans
23 Jun
This is an annual bonfire and beach party held on Amager Beach on Sankt Hans Night.

4 Malmö Pride Festival
Aug ■ www.malmopride.com
Across the bridge, this jamboree was previously called the Rainbow Festival.

5 Copenhagen Pride Festival
Aug ■ www.copenhagenpride.dk
This is a week-long festival held in August. Festivities include the gay pride parade.

6 Mix Copenhagen Film Festival
Oct ■ www.mixcopenhagen.dk
Ten-day lesbian, gay, bi and trans film festival held annually in October.

7 World Aids Day
1 Dec
Commemorated each year.

8 Nordic Open
30 Dec ■ www.pandans.dk/nordic
A popular dance contest for same-sex couples held each year.

9 GAY CPH App
For more events while exploring the city, download this free app.

10 Pan Idræt
www.panidraet.dk
Gay and lesbian sports club for a variety of activites, including badminton, swimming and rugby.

TOP 10 Restaurants

Asian-inspired furniture and tropical flowers at Kiin Kiin

1 Relæ
Talented chef Christian Puglisi was the first Noma-alumnus to make it big, earning his own Michelin star. Diners flock to this minimal space *(see p83)* in Nørrebro to experience an affordable yet remarkable balance of flavours and textures in a completely unfussy environment.

2 Aamann's 1921
Copenhagen's *smørrebrød* (open sandwich) king serves arguably the best sandwiches in town, and reinvents Danish dinner by remixing the usual inputs in unusual combinations. From fried chicken with lingonberries to shrimp on toast made from house-ground flour, this kitchen *(see p75)* is rewardingly obsessed with detail.

3 Kadeau
Everything served at this relaxed yet beautifully designed spot *(see p97)* in Christianshavn is grown on the fertile Danish island Bornholm. The impressive, seasonal 15-course menu deftly weaves foraged botanical delicacies, such as woodruff and wild carrots, into unforgettable unions with the finest seafood and meat.

4 Kiin Kiin
Dining at Europe's only Michelin-starred Thai restaurant *(see p83)* is a feast for the senses. Start by sipping Champagne and scoffing street food in the underground snug, and then follow your nose upstairs to the lemongrass and bamboo-scented dining room for a masterclass in modern Thai cooking.

5 Era Ora
This Michelin-star eatery *(see p97)* has been hailed as the world's best Italian restaurant outside of Italy, and the best restaurant of 2017, by respected foodie magazine *Gambero Rosso*. Ingredients are imported from Italy for authenticity, and prepared according to time-honoured tradition. The impressive wine cellar, meanwhile, houses some 75,000 bottles and 700 labels.

6 Formel B
Beautifully prepared, French-style cuisine using fresh Danish ingredients is the key to the tasty dishes served in this charming restaurant *(see p91)*, which prides itself on supporting animal welfare and sustainability. Sample raw marinated shrimps with squid and soy-ginger browned butter.

Pretty plate at Formel B

7 Noma

Ranked the world's best restaurant four times, Noma *(see p97)* has helped put New Nordic cuisine on the world map. The menu is divided into three seasons, each dramatically different and with its own unique ingredients. It is located amidst nature in hip Refshaleøen and boasts an urban farm. The restaurant offers a special table for students as well. Book in advance.

8 108

Sister restaurant to Noma, 108 earned its own stars by pushing the flavour boundaries of Nordic gastronomy. With reasonable prices and a cool perch on the canal, 108 and its adjoining café, which serves coffee, wine and small plates, are buzzing all day.

Tables at Kong Hans Kælder

9 Kong Hans Kælder

This unique restaurant *(see p75)* is set in Copenhagen's oldest building, offering a wonderful atmosphere beneath its vaulted ceiling. Choose to eat from either the à la carte or fixed-price menu and watch the skilled chef at work in the open kitchen.

10 Søllerød Kro

This Michelin-star countryside inn *(see p105)* is a wonderful retreat away from the hubbub of central Copenhagen. The beautiful interiors are matched by a standout menu that once more highlights the Danes' creative flair with flavours. A tasting menu is available with carefully chosen wine pairings.

TOP 10 DANISH CAFÉS AND BARS

The quirky Laundromat Café

1 Laundromat Café
MAP C3 ▪ Elmegade 15, Nørrebro
Enjoy a coffee while doing your laundry.

2 Coffee Collective
MAP H3 ▪ Vendersgade 6D
From farmer, to roaster, to barista, the Collective crafts the ultimate coffee.

3 Mad og Kaffe
MAP C6 ▪ Sønder Boulevard 68
The most popular café in the city is famous for colourful brunches.

4 Bo-Bi Bar
MAP J4 ▪ Klareboderne 4
Since 1917, artists and office drones have visited this tiny room to talk beer.

5 Øl & Bread
MAP C5 ▪ Viktoriagade 6
This "beer & bread" bar matches its impressive *smørrebrød* line-up to rotating taps of Mikkeller beers.

6 Ruby
MAP J5 ▪ Nybrogade 10
One of the world's top 50 cocktail bars, situated on the canal.

7 La Glace
MAP H4 ▪ Skoubogade 3–5
La Glace is one of the foremost confectioneries in Copenhagen.

8 Brus
MAP C3 ▪ Guldbergsgade 29
This quirky little café roasts all of its beans on the premises.

9 The Corner
MAP M4 ▪ Strandgade 108
Gorgeous house-made pastries and coffee each morning; New Nordic small plates and wine by day.

10 Lidkoeb
MAP C5 ▪ Vesterbrogade 72B
Drinking den in a former apothecary; cocktail bar and whisky house.

Shopping Districts

1 Kronprinsensgade
MAP J4

This posh shopping area includes many of Scandinavia's top designer brands, such as Stig P and Le-Fix. You will also find Scandinavia's oldest tea shop, Perch's Tea Room.

2 Off Strøget (South)
MAP J4–J5

The streets to the south of Strøget are great for "alternative" shopping. Læderstræde and Kompagnistræde are especially good, the latter mostly for its antique shops.

3 Off Strøget (North)
MAP H4–J4

Heading up north from Strøget, you will find numerous little boutiques, record stores and second-hand shops. Go shopping on streets like Skindergade, Larsbjørnstræde, Vestergade and Studiestræde.

4 Strøget
MAP H5–K4

Copenhagen's shopping street is known as "the walking street". The shops, which stretch across five linked pedestrian streets, range from cheerful and inexpensive outlets to designer and upmarket department stores (towards Kongens Nytorv), with something for everyone.

Airy interior of the Fisketorvet mall

5 Fisketorvet Copenhagen Mall
MAP D6 ■ Kalvebod Brygge 59, Havneholmen 5, Vesterbro ■ 33 36 64 00 ■ Open 10am–8pm daily

On the waterfront facing the Inner Harbour, this city mall is minutes away from the Copencabana harbour pool. It has more than 120 shops, several restaurants and a cinema.

6 Vesterbro
MAP C5–C6

This former red-light area is now an offbeat shopping district offering some very good bargains. Among

Window-shopping along Copenhagen's famous shopping street, Strøget

the more interesting streets in the neighbourhood are Istedgade, which is lined with boutiques and art shops, and Værnedamsvej, which has several independent fashion stores and gourmet food shops.

7 Nansensgade
MAP G3

Located on the outskirts of the old town, this area has a mix of traditional and trendy boutiques, as well as good restaurants and cafés.

8 Torvehallerne KBH
MAP H3

Food-lovers sure are in for a treat at Copenhagen's covered market on Israels Plads. On offer here are a variety of gourmet food stands as well as takeout delights and some delicious delis.

Seafood stall at Torvehallerne KBH

9 Nørrebro
MAP C3–D3

Not as trendy as it once was, but Nørrebro still has many second-hand stores and chic boutiques. Head to Ravnsborggade for antiques, Jaegersborggade for the offbeat and Elmegade for vintage clothes.

10 Bredgade
MAP L3

If you are looking for traditional, pre-20th-century antiques, this is the perfect place to visit. Here you will find several grand-looking shops and auction houses that sell all kinds of antiques, including authentic paintings and statues.

TOP 10 DANISH DESIGN COMPANIES

Georg Jensen Silverware

1 Georg Jensen Silverware
www.georgjensen.com
Original, organic tableware designs and casual jewellery.

2 Cylinda-Line (by Arne Jacobsen)
www.stelton.dk
Popular tableware collection (1967) in steel, wood and plastic.

3 Bang & Olufsen
www.bang-olufsen.com
Known for their cutting-edge audio-visual designs.

4 Kaare Klint Furniture
Combines ergonomics with elegant 18th-century English styles.

5 Bodum
www.bodum.com
Classic and smart kitchenware in steel and glass.

6 LEGO®
www.lego.com
These popular building blocks were introduced in 1952.

7 Vipp
www.vipp.com
Designers of a classic stainless steel pedal bin, Vipp's products also include soap dishes and dispensers.

8 Royal Copenhagen
www.royalcopenhagen.com
Royal porcelain design featuring famous Flora Danica motifs.

9 Poul Henningsen Lamps
Lamp design creating the effect of maximum light and minimum shadow.

10 Kjærholm Furniture
Poul Kjærholm-designed functional coffee tables and chairs, all named simply PK with a number. Production continues under the leadership of his son, Thomas.

TOP10 Copenhagen for Free

The Royal Botanical Gardens

1 Botanisk Have

Take a stroll through this green oasis *(see p78)* in the heart of the city, which boasts stunning glasshouses, gardens and over 13,000 species of plantlife. Behind the scenes, the garden's botanists develop scientific collections of rare plants and fungi, making them available for research, teaching and the public.

2 Visit world-class museums

www.natmus.dk
All of the city's national museums, including Nationalmuseet *(see pp32–3)* and the SMK – National Gallery of Denmark *(see pp26–7)*, are free for under-18s, while many city-centre institutions offer free entry for adults one day per week – check the relevant website for specific days.

3 Watch an open-air movie

MAP D2 ■ Edel Sauntes Allé
■ www.zulu.dk
It doesn't get much more cosy and *hygge* than this: every summer, Zulu brings its open–air cinema to Fælledparken, a sprawling public park in Østerbro. All you need to do is bring a blanket.

4 Havnebadet

MAP E6 ■ Islands Brygge 14
■ www.teambade.kk.dk
On hot days, Copenhageners flock to this open-air swimming bath. There are five pools in all, while three diving towers give thrillseekers the opportunity to show off their stunts.

5 A Harbourside Promenade

Make the obligatory visit to the Little Mermaid *(see p13)* on foot, and then continue inland into Kastellet, the historic green fortress that is still a working military barracks, before exploring the Gefion Fountain and St Alban's Church *(see p80)*.

6 Den Sorte Diamant

MAP K5 ■ Søren Kierkegaards Plads 1
Not only does this eye-catching modern extension of the Royal Library house every book ever printed in Danish (some six million), it's also home to the very good National Museum of Photography.

7 Changing of the guard at Amalienborg Palace

Come rain or shine, the Royal Life Guards stoically stand watch outside Amalienborg Palace *(see pp24–5)*. Every day at noon, you can watch them march through the city.

8 Christiansborg Tårnet

At 106 m (348 ft), the tower on Christiansborg Palace *(see pp30–31)* is the highest point in Copenhagen's historic centre, and offers great views of the city. Space on the viewing platform is limited, so expect to queue for the elevator.

9 Explore Christiania

A maze of hippy hangouts and Hobbit-like homes, this self-declared "freetown" *(see pp28–9)* has been a counter-culture haven for dreamers and anarchists for over 40 years.

Communal area in Christiania

10 Absalon

MAP C6 ▪ Sønder Blvd 73
▪ **Open 7am–midnight daily ▪ www.absaloncph.dk**

Hang out with locals at this centre offering free activities for all the family. Show off your ping-pong prowess, dance the tango or try some traditional Danish cooking.

Guards outside Amalienborg Palace

TOP 10 BUDGET TIPS

Street food outlet

1 Try street food
Fast-food outlets are plentiful, and street-food outlets offer substantial, high-quality dishes for 100 Dkr or less.

2 Get Outdoors
Walking the streets is free and fascinating, while public parks and gardens (except Tivoli) are free, and often host free entertainment.

3 See a free concert
MAP H5 ▪ Vesterbrogade 3
Tivoli *(see p14)* has a summer concert series often with international artists. Free with park admission every Friday.

4 Buy a Copenhagen Card
The Copenhagen Card offers transport and sightseeing discounts *(see p112)*.

5 Free walking tours
There are several walking tour operators that provide expert tips as well as sight information. A tip is expected at the end of the tour.

6 Have a big breakfast
Eat-all-you-want breakfasts offer good value for money, even at 100–150 Dkr.

7 Don't worry about tipping
Tips are usually included in bills at restaurants, hotels and taxis.

8 Free outdoor concerts
Every Wednesday in the spring and summer, students from the Royal Danish Academy of Music perform classical concerts at the Teatermuseet.

9 Try ice-skating
Skate for free in the winter at rinks in Toftegård Plads in Valby, Frederiksberg Runddel and Blågårds Plads.

10 Dine outside
Barbecues, picnics and alcohol are allowed in most public parks across Copenhagen, ideal for dining alfresco.

Copenhagen
Area by Area

A view across the striking rooftops
of Copenhagen's old city

TOP 10 Tivoli North to Gothersgade

Rich in history and culture, this area is a popular entertainment destination. Heading northeast of Tivoli, which was originally outside the city walls, you can walk back in time through the old town that evolved during the Middle Ages – though much of it succumbed to fire in the 18th century – to Slotsholmen, the site where the first dwellings that became the city of Copenhagen were built in the 12th century. Along the way, you will find great shopping areas, museums, an old town and a truly wonderful royal palace.

Christian V Statue

TIVOLI NORTH TO GOTHERSGADE

Astronomical clock on display

1 Astronomical Clock
MAP H5 ■ Rådhus,
Rådhuspladsen 1 ■ 33 66 25 86
■ Open 9am–5pm Mon–Fri,
10am–1pm Sat ■ Adm

This clock shows local time, solar
time, sunrise and sunset times,
celestial pole movement and the
movement of the planets.

Top 10 Sights
see pp69–71

Places to Eat
see p75

Shops
see p73

The Best of the Rest
see p72

Nightlife
see p74

2 Kunstforeningen Gammel Strand
MAP J4 ■ Gammel Strand 48 ■ 33 36
02 60 ■ Open 11am–5pm Tue–Sun
(until 8pm Wed) ■ Adm; free with
Copenhagen Card ■ www.glstrand.dk

The Gammel Strand art association
was formed in 1825. The centre puts
on five to six changing exhibitions
annually, from group shows to retro-
spectives, both classic and contemporary. There is also an excellent
bookshop on the first floor and
a pleasant café. To gain disabled
access you must walk through
the courtyard at Læderstræde 15.

3 Tivoli
A park that is now almost
synonymous with Copenhagen,
Tivoli *(see pp14–15)* should be high
on the list for any visitor to the city.
In any season, this park buzzes with
the sounds of exhilarating rides. It
is not only for adventure-seekers
though. At night, the setting turns
quite magical and romantic, with
fairy lights and Japanese lanterns
glowing in the darkness. There's
often live music, too.

Flowers in bloom at Tivoli

4 Latin Quarter
To the west of Strøget lies
the Latin Quarter *(see pp18–19)*, the
original home of the University of
Copenhagen. It dates back to the
Middle Ages when the primary language of education was Latin. Some
of the old university buildings are
used, although much of the campus
is now on the island of Amager.

5 Amagertorv
MAP J4

This busy square (see p62) is in the middle of Strøget. Note the attractive tiles designed by Bjørn Nørgaard. The square's focal point, the lovely Storkespringvandet fountain, provided the inspiration for a Danish folk song of the 1960s, and today the fountain is a popular meeting place. The cafés Norden and Europa, on either side of the square, are always buzzing.

6 Slotsholmen

A visit to Slotsholmen could take up almost an entire day, as there is plenty to see. It is primarily the site of Christiansborg Slot (see pp30–31), which burnt down in 1794, but was rebuilt and is now home to Denmark's Parliament; it is also used by the Queen for State functions (visit the State Rooms on a guided tour). Museums here include the Danish War Museum, filled with historic arms and armour, and the delightful Teatermuseet (see p44) featuring the 18th-century palace theatre. Other sights include the palace church and the 12th-century ruins of the first Copenhagen castle where the city's founder, Bishop Absalon, resided.

7 Ny Carlsberg Glyptotek
MAP H6 ▪ Dantes Plads 7
▪ 33 41 81 41 ▪ Open 11am–6pm Tue–Sun (until 10pm Thu) ▪ Adm; free with Copenhagen Card ▪ www. glyptoteket.com

This superb art gallery is home to a diverse collection of Mediterranean, classical and Egyptian art and artifacts. Danish and

Statues at Ny Carlsberg Glyptotek

19th-century French works of art are also on display, including splendid French Impressionist paintings (see p44). The museum is housed in a 19th-century building with a cupola, beneath which lies an indoor winter garden, sculptures and water features. The modern wing is a wonderful area filled with light.

8 Rådhus
MAP H5 ▪ Rådhuspladsen 1
▪ 33 66 25 86 ▪ Open 9am–4pm Mon–Fri, 9:30am–1pm Sat ▪ Tours in English at 1pm Mon–Fri, 10am Sat; tower tour 11am & 2pm Mon–Fri, noon Sat ▪ Adm for tours and tower

The Rådhus, or town hall, is a mock-Gothic building replete with fantastical sea creatures, built between 1892 and 1905 and designed by architect Martin Nyrop. Its tower affords superb views of the city. Take a tour, or just pop in to

Copenhagen's Rådhus

see the pre-Raphaelitesque entrance way, or the Italianate reception hall. Many Copenhageners get married here, so you may see several wedding parties on the town hall steps.

9 Nationalmuseet

The National Museum (see pp32–3) is housed inside a former royal residence, dating from the 18th century. The exhibits trace Danish history , from ancient times to the present, including some amazing ethnographic collections. The most popular exhibits at the museum chart the history of Danes from the Ice Age to the Viking campaigns.

10 Kongens Nytorv and Nyhavn

At the top of Nyhavn stands Kongens Nytorv or the King's New Square (see pp22–3), an elegant area surrounded by fashionable 18th-century mansions that house upmarket department stores, banks and hotels. The picturesque square is flanked by a number of prominent institutions such as Charlottenborg Slot (now an exhibition space and home to the academy of art) and Det Kongelige Teater or Royal Theatre. Nyhavn (meaning "new harbour") is a lively area filled with restaurants, cafés and old sailing boats along the canal quayside. The atmosphere here is a stark contrast to what it was in the 1670s, when sailors, traders and low-lives frequented the area. When Hans Christian Andersen lived here it was a red-light district. Even until the 1970s, this was not a part of town that many would have visited at night.

A WALKING TOUR OF THE AREA

▶ MORNING

Start your day's ramble at the **Ny Carlsberg Glyptotek**; don't miss the impressive Egyptian and Impressionist collections. Have an early lunch at the museum's charming Winter Garden Café (Dantes Plads 7).

AFTERNOON

After lunch, cross H C Andersen Boulevard and head to the **Nationalmuseet** to take one of the hour-long tours. Stroll to the end of Ny Vestergade until you reach Frederiks Kanal. Cross the bridge and spend some time at **Christiansborg Slot** (see pp30–31). If you arrive by 2pm, pop into the stables, the **Teatermuseet** (see p44) and the ruins before taking a tour of the State Rooms at 3pm. Then, walk back over the bridge and turn right onto Gammel Strand (note the **Fiskerkone**, see p41) for afternoon snacks at one of the restaurants and cafés. Walk down **Købmagergade** via Højbro Plads, right up to **Rundetårn** (see pp18–19). If you are feeling energetic, hike to the top for a good view of the city. Heading back down, take a left on to **Strøget** and keep walking until you reach **Kongens Nytorv and Nyhavn** – a perfect spot for an evening drink and supper at one of the quayside restaurants and bars. Instead of heading back via Strøget, take the less mainstream **Læderstræde**. Walk to **Rådhuspladsen** and go across to **Tivoli** (see pp14–15). Spend the evening at these lovely gardens enjoying the atmosphere.

See map on pp68–9

The Best of the Rest

1 Caritas Springvandet
MAP H4 ■ Gammel Torv

Dating back to 1608, the Charity Fountain is one of the city's oldest.

2 Københavns Museum
MAP H5 ■ Stormgade 18 ■ See website for opening times ■ Adm ■ www.cphmuseum.kk.dk

The City Museum takes visitors on a journey through urban history, from the original settlers to today.

Caritas Fountain

3 Rådhuspladsen
MAP H5

At the end of Strøget, the town hall square is one of the liveliest areas.

4 Strøget
MAP H5–K4

This is the name given to the five main, interconnected shopping streets (see p62) of Copenhagen.

5 Guinness World Records Museum
MAP K4 ■ Østergade 16 ■ 33 32 31 31 ■ Open Sep–mid-Jun: 10am–6pm daily (until 8pm Fri & Sat); mid-Jun–Aug: 10am–10pm daily ■ Adm (combined tickets available) ■ www.ripleys.com/copenhagen

As the name suggests, 500 Guinness World Records are displayed here (see p52).

6 World of H C Andersen Museum
MAP H5 ■ Rådhuspladsen 57 ■ 33 32 31 31 ■ Open Sep–mid-Jun: 10am–6pm daily (until 8pm Fri–Sat); mid-Jun–Aug: 10am–10pm daily ■ Adm ■ www.ripleys.com/copenhagen

Scenes from Andersen's fairy tales are found here, plus other memorabilia.

7 Grand Teatret
MAP H5 ■ Mikkel Bryggers Gade 8 ■ 33 15 16 11 ■ www.grandteatret.dk

A historic six-screen cinema with some incredibly comfy seats and an excellent café, this is the film buffs' go-to place for international and arthouse movies.

8 Statue of H C Andersen
MAP H5 ■ H C Andersens Boulevard

This statue of the author by Henry Lukow-Nielsen dates from 1961.

9 Georg Jensen Museum
MAP J4 ■ Amagertorv 4 ■ 33 14 02 29 ■ Open 10am–6pm Mon–Thu, 10am–7pm Fri, 10am–5pm Sat (Jun–Sep: Sun) ■ www.georgjensen.com

The jewellery and homeware of the famous silversmith are on display at this wonderful museum.

10 Gammel Strand
MAP J4

This canalside street is home to excellent restaurants, one of the city's best flea markets and the Kunstforeningen Gammel Strand (see p69), an admirable art museum. It is also a pick-up point for Stromma Canal Tours (see p13).

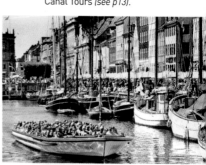
People enjoying a Stromma Canal Tour

Shops

1 Illums Bolighus
MAP J4 ▪ Amagertorv 10 ▪ 33
14 19 41 ▪ www.illumsbolighus.dk
This shrine to stylish interior design
and kitchenware (mainly Italian and
Danish) offers everything from Royal
Copenhagen porcelain to groovy dog-
biscuit dispensers and objets d'art.

2 Georg Jensen
MAP J4 ▪ Amagertorv 4 ▪ 33
11 40 80 ▪ www.georgjensen.com
Superb designs from the historic
firm of George Jensen are available
at its flagship store. These include a
range of stylish jewellery, watches,
cutlery, candlesticks, antiques and
designer sunglasses.

3 ILLUM
MAP K4 ▪ Østergade 52
▪ 33 14 40 02 ▪ www.illum.dk
A stylish, six-storeyed department
store offering quality clothing and
homeware. There are also several
cafés, a bakery and a supermarket.

4 Birger Christensen
MAP K4 ▪ Østergade 38
▪ 33 11 55 55 ▪ www.birger-
christensen.com
This fashion store sells Birger
Christensen coats and jackets, as
well as international labels.

5 Royal Copenhagen Porcelain
MAP J4 ▪ Amagertorv 6
▪ 33 13 71 81 ▪ www.
royalcopenhagen.com
This flagship store offers a
range of designs, from the
classic 18th-century flora
danica design to the
modern and organic.

**A Royal Copenhagen
fruit bowl**

6 Mads Nørgaard
MAP J4 ▪ Amagertov 15 ▪ 33
32 01 28 ▪ www.madsnorgaard.com
Classic, casual Danish menswear
is sold here, including the timeless
trademark unisex striped top.

7 Noa Noa
MAP K4 ▪ Østergade 6 ▪ 29
74 31 66 ▪ www.noanoa.com/fr_fr
A contemporary Danish label that
offers women's cottons, linens and
silks in quirky, pretty styles. They
also do a similar collection for girls
aged 3–12.

Accessories on display at Hay House

8 Hay House
MAP J4 ▪ Østergade 61, 2nd
Floor ▪ 42 82 08 20 ▪ www.hay.dk
In addition to the store on
Pilestræde, a larger branch has
opened above Café Norden on
Amagertorv. Filled with bright plastic
furniture and accessories.

9 A Pair
MAP K4
▪ Ny Østergade 3
▪ 33 91 99 20
▪ www.apair.dk
Here you will find
fashionable footwear for men
and women, as well as
leather bags and belts
with large silver buckles.
It is a chain with shops
all over Denmark.

10 Sand
MAP K4 ▪ Østergade 40 ▪ 33
14 21 21 ▪ www.sand-europe.com
This Danish fashion house offers
stylish and classic clothing and
accessories for men and women.

See map on pp68–9

Nightlife

The cigar lounge at stylish restaurant The Jane

① Ruby
MAP J5 ▪ Nybrogade 10 ▪ 33 93 12 03 ▪ Open 4pm–2am Mon– Sat, 6pm–2am Sun ▪ www.rby.dk

This exclusive bar is styled as an old-fashioned gentlemen's club.

② Level
MAP H4 ▪ Nørregade 1 ▪ 33 11 74 78 ▪ Open 11pm–6am Fri & Sat ▪ www.levelcph.dk

The entrance fee for this 1930s-style club includes unlimited soft drinks and draught beer.

③ Jazzhus Montmartre
MAP K3 ▪ Store Regnegade 19A ▪ 70 26 32 67 ▪ Open 5:30– 11:30pm Thu–Sat; concerts start at 8pm ▪ Book ahead ▪ Adm ▪ www.jazzhusmontmartre.dk

A legendary jazz venue that attracts world-class jazz musicians.

④ Hard Rock Cafe
MAP H5 ▪ Rådhuspladsen 45–47 ▪ 33 12 43 33 ▪ www.hardrock.com

This international chain has live music and features memorabilia from artists such as Metallica, The Rolling Stones, Amy Winehouse and Michael Jackson.

⑤ Studenterhuset
MAP J3 ▪ Købmagergade 52 ▪ www.studenterhuset.com

This bar serves beer at discounted prices, and hosts local bands.

⑥ The Jane
MAP J4 ▪ Gråbrødretorv 8 ▪ 61 69 21 64 ▪ From 8pm onwards Thu– Sat (from 4pm Fri) ▪ www.thejane.dk

Step into a Mad Men-esque world at this city-centre speakeasy.

⑦ Strøm
MAP J4 ▪ Niels Hemmingsens Gade 32 ▪ 81 18 94 21 ▪ Open 6pm– midnight Mon–Thu, 6pm–2am Fri & Sat ▪ www.strombar.dk

This spit 'n' sawdust speakeasy serves up twists on classic cocktails.

⑧ Alice
MAP J4 ▪ Niels Hemmingsens Gade 10 ▪ 33 15 47 00 ▪ Open from 7pm for concerts only ▪ www.alicecph.com

A live jazz venue attracting both international and local bands.

⑨ 1105
MAP K4 ▪ Kristen Bernikows Gade 4 ▪ 33 93 11 05 ▪ Open 7pm– 2am Wed & Thu, 4pm–2am Fri & Sat ▪ www.1105.dk

The bartenders at this hip cocktail bar mix the best drinks in the city.

⑩ Club Mambo
MAP H5 ▪ Vester Voldgade 85 ▪ 33 11 97 66 ▪ Open 8:30pm–11pm Tue, 8:30pm–3am Thu, 10pm–5am Fri & Sat ▪ www.clubmambo.dk

Dance to salsa in this popular club.

→ See map on pp68–9

Places to Eat

PRICE CATEGORIES

For a three-course meal for one without alcohol, including taxes and charges.

Ⓚ under 300 Dkr ⓀⓀ 300–500 Dkr
ⓀⓀⓀ Over 500 Dkr

1 Aamann's 1921

MAP J4 ▪ Niels Hemmingsens Gade 19–21 ▪ 20 80 52 04 ▪ Open 11:30am–10pm daily ▪ www. aamanns.dk/aamanns-1921 ▪ ⓀⓀ

Rooted in traditional Danish fare, Aamann's (see p60) offers an innovative interpretation of the classic Danish *smørrebrød*.

2 L'Alsace

MAP K4 ▪ Ny Østergade 9 ▪ 33 14 57 43 ▪ Open 11:30am–midnight Mon–Sat ▪ Closed Sun & public holidays ▪ www. alsace.dk ▪ ⓀⓀ

Smorgasbord at Aamann's 1921

This classy restaurant specializes in dishes from Alsace, with an emphasis on fresh fish and seafood.

3 Kong Hans Kælder

MAP K4 ▪ Vingårdsstræde 6 ▪ 33 11 68 68 ▪ Open 6pm–midnight Wed–Sat D ▪ www.konghans.dk ▪ ⓀⓀⓀ

This historic restaurant is in the city's oldest building. The menu is gourmet and the setting is formal.

4 Geist

MAP K4 ▪ Kongens Nytorv 8 ▪ 33 13 37 13 ▪ www.restaurantgeist. dk ▪ ⓀⓀ

Stylish eatery, both lavish and informal; compose your meal from a long list of small- and medium-sized dishes, including vegetarian options.

5 Atlas Bar

MAP H4 ▪ Larsbjørnsstræde 18 ▪ 33 15 03 52 ▪ Closed Sun ▪ www. atlasbar.dk ▪ ⓀⓀ

Locals head to this cool basement for a wide range of exotic dishes.

6 Krogs Fiskerestaurant

MAP J4 ▪ Gammel Strand 38 ▪ 33 15 89 15 ▪ Closed Sun D ▪ www. krogs.dk ▪ ⓀⓀ

This landmark fish restaurant offers organic and sustainable lunch menus.

7 Tivoli Food Hall

MAP H5 ▪ Vesterbrogade 3 ▪ 33 15 10 01 ▪ Open 11am–11pm daily ▪ www.tivoli.dk ▪ Ⓚ

At the corner of Tivoli, visitors will find a wide selection of food stalls (see p61), each with their own unique take on international dining experiences.

8 Bankeråt

MAP G3 ▪ Ahlefeldtsgade 29 ▪ 33 93 69 88 ▪ www. bankeraat.dk ▪ Ⓚ

Enjoy steaks, salads and beers in this artistic venue.

9 Restaurant Peder Oxe

MAP J4 ▪ Gråbrødretov 11 ▪ 33 11 00 77 ▪ Open 11am–11pm Sun–Wed, 11am–midnight Thu–Sat ▪ www.pederoxe.dk ▪ ⓀⓀ

A well-established restaurant on a picturesque square.

10 Kompasset

MAP L4 ▪ Nyhavn 65 ▪ 44 22 52 22 ▪ www.restaurantkompasset. dk ▪ ⓀⓀ

This restaurant has a *smørrebrød* focus and is the perfect spot for lunch overlooking the harbour.

Outdoor seating at Kompasset

TOP 10 Nørrebro, Østerbro and North of Gothersgade

Of these three neighbourhoods, two are additions to the original Copenhagen site, which took up what is now called the "Inner City". Until the 19th century, this area was mainly farmland; today it is a lively, multicultural part of the city with plenty of bars, cafés and alternative shopping centres. Østerbro, slightly northeast of Nørrebro, has remained an uncluttered, suburban residential area since the 19th century. The area north of Gothersgade is part of the Inner City and takes in later parts of the capital dating back to the Renaissance period.

Vase from the Designmuseum

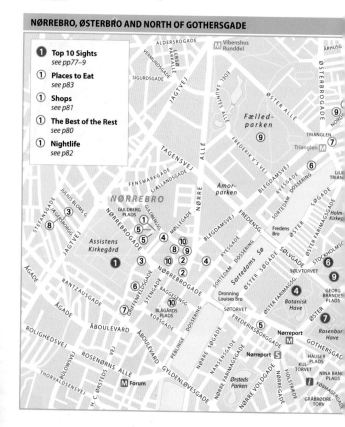

NØRREBRO, ØSTERBRO AND NORTH OF GOTHERSGADE

1. **Top 10 Sights** see pp77–9
1. **Places to Eat** see p83
1. **Shops** see p81
1. **The Best of the Rest** see p80
1. **Nightlife** see p82

1 Assistens Kirkegård

MAP C3 ▪ Kapelvej ▪ 35 37 19 17 ▪ Open Apr–Sep: 7am–10pm daily; Oct–Mar: 7am–7pm daily ▪ www. assistens.dk

If you are not a devoted fan of famous dead Danes, this cemetery may not be top of your list. However, it is a wonderful place to relax or take a romantic walk. The church-yard is beautiful and is located in the gritty Nørrebro district.

2 Marmorkirken

Standing close to Amalienborg is the splendid Marmorkirken or Marble Church (see pp24–5), a part of the great architectural design for the area of Frederiksstaden. However, plans for its construction were so

The splendid Marmorkirken cupola

extravagant that finances ran out and work was abandoned in 1770. For more than a century, it stood as a picturesque ruin before being rescued and financed by a Danish industrialist, and in 1894 the church was finally completed.

3 Amalienborg

Some royal palaces allow visits only during summer weekends. Amalienborg (both Christian VII and Christian VIII's Palaces) and the museum are open to the public year-round. The palaces were built as an important part of the 18th-century aristocratic district Frederiksstaden (see pp24–5) and are very different from the narrow streets and houses of the old quarter. When the complex was first built, it was visually linked to the Marble Church; the Opera House (see pp94–5) and the construction across the harbour on Holmen offer a contemporary visual contrast.

Amalienborg royal palace

The manicured gardens of Botanisk Have

4 Botanisk Have
MAP H2–J2 ▪ Gothersgade 128
▪ Open May–Sep: 8:30am–6pm daily;
Oct–Apr: 8:30am–4pm daily ▪ Adm;
free entrance to the garden ▪ www.
botanik.snm.ku.dk

Among the prettiest outdoor spaces
in Copenhagen, these gardens are
studded with lakes, bridges and
lovely flowerbeds *(see p64)*. Climb
the winding staircase for a great view
of exotic trees below. The grounds
are also home to three museums,
which cover botany, geology and
zoology. By 2021, all three museums
will be under one roof in the gardens.

5 Davids Samling
MAP K3 ▪ Kronprinsessegade
30–32 ▪ 33 73 49 49 ▪ Open 10am–
5pm Tue–Sun (until 9pm Wed)
▪ www.davidmus.dk

This museum holds the private art
collection of Danish Supreme Court
barrister and art lover, C L David. The
fine Islamic collection is Scandinavia's
largest, and includes a fine range of
Islamic art from the 7th to the 19th
centuries. There is also a
collection of 18th- and
19th-century European
decorative arts. The
collection is set in an
elegant 19th-century
town house.

**Statue at
Rosenborg Slot**

6 Den Hirschsprungske Samling
MAP J1 ▪ Stockholmsgade 20 ▪ 35 42
03 36 ▪ Open 11am–4pm Wed–Sun
▪ Adm; free with Copenhagen Card
▪ www.hirschsprung.dk

This small art museum is situated
just behind the SMK and displays
the collection of tobacco magnate
Heinrich Hirschsprung, given to
the nation in 1902. Housed in a
19th-century building, the large
collection is fittingly dedicated to
19th- and early 20th-century Danish
art, including works by painters
of the Golden Age and the North
Jutland colony of Skagen painters,
known for their bright colours
and luminous treatment of light.
Contemporary furniture is also
displayed in the museum.

7 Rosenborg Slot and Kongens Have
Rosenborg Castle and the King's
Garden *(see p16–17)* are among the
highlights of the city, especially
on sunny days when the park is
full of people and entertainment.
Rosenborg Slot was built in
1606–34 and is the only castle
in the city centre that has
not succumbed to fire.
Little has changed
about the structure
since the time the
royals inhabited it in
the 17th century.

8 Frihedsmuseet

MAP L2 ■ Churchill-parken 7
■ 33 47 39 21 ■ Closed until May 2020
■ www.natmus.dk

The Museum of Danish Resistance pays tribute to, and tells the stories of, the people who lived in Denmark during the time of German occupation (1940–45). It explores their resistance activities, ranging from underground newspapers and radio stations to sabotage and the rescue of virtually every Jew in Denmark from under the noses of the Germans. The museum is closed due to fire damage and is likely to reopen in May 2020.

9 SMK – National Gallery of Denmark

The SMK (see pp26–7) has a collection of both national and international art, including works by the Old Masters and modern icons.

Art at the SMK

10 Designmuseum Danmark

MAP L2 ■ Bredgade 68 ■ 33 18 56 56 ■ Open 10am–6pm Tue–Sun (until 9pm Wed) ■ Adm; free with Copenhagen Card ■ www.design museum.dk

Dedicated entirely to the art of design, this museum (see p44) is housed in a splendid 18th-century Rococo building. The collection comprises everything from Danish-designed colanders and cardboard chairs to posters, textiles and Chinese decorative arts.

A WALK NORTH OF GOTHERSGADE

MORNING

Start your day among the Impressionistic paintings of the Danish Skagen colony of painters at the **Den Hirschsprungske Samling** museum. Then cross the gardens to the impressive **SMK – National Gallery of Denmark**; take an audio guide to learn about the displays.

AFTERNOON

For lunch, stop at either the museum café or the **Botanisk Have** café, depending upon the weather. The gardens are a great place for a picnic, too. Don't forget to visit the Palm House. Heading out from the gate on Gothersgade turn onto Øster Voldgade, cross over to **Rosenborg Slot**. Spend a few enjoyable hours here, visiting the castle, the crown jewels and strolling through the gardens.

Afterwards leave from the Kronprinsessegade gate and pop into **Davids Samling** to see some Islamic art. Walk down Dronningens Tværgade, take a left onto Bredgade and walk right up to **Marmorkirken** (see p77). If you are here by 1pm, take a tour up the tower. Right in front of the church is **Amalienborg** (see p77). Take a walk through it to the pretty banks of the harbour and see the **Opera House** (see p94) across the water. If you are up for a 20-minute walk, head towards **The Little Mermaid** (see p80), passing Gefionspringvandet (see p80) and **Frihedsmuseet** (temporarily closed). To get back to town, hop onto the No. 26 bus from Folke Bernadottes Allé.

See map on pp76–7

The Best of the Rest

1 Gefionspringvandet
MAP M2 ▪ Langelinie

This bronze statue is a dramatic sight, representing the tale of the goddess Gefion as she ploughs enough land to create the island of Zealand, on which Copenhagen is found.

The bronze statue of goddess Gefion

2 Medicinsk Museion
MAP L2 ▪ Bredgade 62 ▪ 35 32 38 00 ▪ Open 10am–4pm Tue–Fri, noon–4pm Sat–Sun ▪ Guided tour in English 2pm Tue–Fri, 1:30pm Sat–Sun ▪ Adm ▪ www.museion.ku.dk

The Medical Museum of Copenhagen University has exhibits dating back to the 18th century.

3 The Little Mermaid (Den Lille Havfrue)
MAP M1 ▪ Langelinie, top of Kastellet

This statue of the heroine of Hans Christian Andersen's fairy tale, *The Little Mermaid (see p13)*, perched on a rock in the harbour, has been staring out to sea since 1913.

4 Amaliehaven
Filled with box hedges and fountains, this modern park *(see p24)* lies to the east of Amalienborg, facing the harbour, with views of the Opera House.

5 Alexander Nevsky Kirke
MAP L3 ▪ Bredgade 53 ▪ 33 13 60 46 ▪ Open 10am–noon daily

This Russian Orthodox church (1883) was a gift from Tsar Alexander III to celebrate his marriage to the Danish Princess Marie Dagmar.

6 Kastelskirken
MAP L1 ▪ Kastellet ▪ 33 15 65 58 ▪ Open 8am–6pm Mon–Fri

The military church at Kastellet has been holding services here since the 17th century.

7 St Alban's Church
MAP M2 ▪ Churchillparken 11 ▪ 33 11 85 18 ▪ Open to visitors in summer, 10am–4pm Mon–Sat, 1–4pm Sun ▪ www.st-albans.dk

St Alban's is Denmark's only Anglican church and is a Neo-Gothic building dating from 1885.

8 Kongelige Afstøbningssamling
MAP M2 ▪ Toldbodgade 40 ▪ 33 74 84 84 ▪ Open for special events ▪ www.smk.dk

The Royal Cast Collection is heralded on the harbour with a replica of Michelangelo's statue of *David*.

9 Fælledparken
MAP D2

Copenhagen's largest park *(see p53)* is where the city gathers for the annual 1 May springtime celebrations.

10 Kastellet
MAP L1 ▪ 72 81 11 41 ▪ Only grounds open to visitors

This pentagram-shaped fortress was constructed as protection against the Swedes, but was only ever used against the English in 1807.

A cannon on show at Kastellet

Shops

1 Nyhavns Glaspusteri
MAP L4 ▪ Toldbodgade 4 ▪ 40
17 01 34 ▪ www.copenhagenglass.dk
This charming glass gallery is where
glass-blower Christian Edwards
sculpts and sells his creations.

2 Divaen og Krudtuglen
MAP C3 ▪ Elmegade 22 ▪ 26
71 59 68 ▪ www.millou.dk
Bright clothes and shoes for kids
and mums alike, as well as trays of
cute, inexpensive toys. Look out for
the ecofriendly labelled brands.

3 Sneakers & Coffee
▪ Jægersborggade 30 ▪ 42
57 67 89 ▪ Closed Sun
Indulge your sneaker craze at this
hip shop stocking rare kicks such
as retro Adidas and Finnish Karhus.
The coffee bar keeps shoppers
amped during fittings.

**4 Tage Andersen Boutique
& Museum**
MAP K4 ▪ Ny Adelgade 12 ▪ 33 93 09
13 ▪ Adm ▪ www.tage-andersen.com
Run by flower artist and designer
Tage Andersen, this flower shop,
gallery and museum is full of lovely
and unique arrangements. To see
the whole place you'll need to climb
up a steep staircase.

5 Eco Ego
MAP H3 ▪ Nørre Farimagsgade
82 ▪ 32 12 06 12 ▪ www.ecoego.dk
Denmark's first fair-trade, organic
lifestyle shop sells everything from
shoes and skincare products to
games. There's a good selection of
eco and ethical products for children.

6 Brund
MAP E2 ▪ Nordre Frihavnsgade
49 ▪ 35 43 51 33 ▪ www.brund.dk
Raw denim and bench-made boots
line the shelves of this rugged
menswear shop, which stocks a
selection of high-end goods from
brands including Loake, John
Smedley and Crockett & Jones.

Interior of Normann Copenhagen

7 Normann Copenhagen
MAP E2 ▪ Østerbrogade 70
▪ 35 27 05 40 ▪ www.normann-
copenhagen.com
This vast warehouse housed in an
old cinema sells designer furniture,
clothes and interior design items.

8 Susanne Juul
MAP K3 ▪ Store Kongensgade
14 ▪ 33 32 25 22 ▪ Closed Sun & Mon
▪ www.susannejuul.dk
Suppliers of glamorous, ornate hats
to royalty and celebrities.

9 Dag & Hammar
MAP E2 ▪ Nordre Frihavnsgade
19 ▪ 31 37 77 20
This smart men's boutique also
stocks threads from the likes of
Fred Perry and Amor Lux, as well
as Clark's Originals shoes.

10 Mondo Kaos
MAP C3 ▪ Birkegade 1 ▪ 60
95 11 36 ▪ www.mondokaos.dk
New versions of vintage clothes,
including retro 1950s-style dresses,
are on the racks of this colourful
rockabilly boutique.

See map on pp76–7

Nightlife

1 BRUS
MAP C3 ▪ Guldbergsgade 29F
▪ 75 22 22 00 ▪ www.tapperietbrus.dk
With 33 draft beers and an in-house bottleshop, there's plenty to keep even the thirstiest beer lover interested at this Nørrebro brewpub.

The elegant BRUS bar

2 Gefährlich
MAP C3 ▪ Fælledvej 7 ▪ 35 24 13 24 ▪ Closed Mon & Sun ▪ www.gefahrlich.dk
This is one of the area's most popular bars (see p57). It also has a good restaurant and live music.

3 Bodega
MAP C3 ▪ Kapelvej 1 ▪ 35 39 07 07 ▪ www.bodega.dk
This popular pre-clubbing venue serves good bar food. DJ sessions are held on Fridays and Saturdays.

4 The Barking Dog
MAP D3 ▪ Sankt Hans Gade 19 ▪ 35 36 16 00 ▪ www.thebarkingdog.dk
This wallet-friendly cocktail bar is a hit with students and hipsters alike, where mixologists spin classic funk and soul records while they create weird, wonderful drinks.

5 Empire Bio Cinema
MAP C3 ▪ Guldbergsgade 29F ▪ 35 36 00 36 ▪ www.empirebio.dk
This comfortable arts cinema holds good programmes and has a cosy bar and café area.

6 Søernes Ølbar
MAP E2 ▪ Sortedam Dossering 83 ▪ 32 19 63 80 ▪ www.soernesoelbar.dk
A lakeside craft-beer joint with an impeccable selection of draft and bottled ales, porters and sours, this is a haven for hopheads on the hunt for rare and obscure brews.

7 DuPong
MAP C4 ▪ Griffenfeldsgade 52 ▪ www.dupong.dk
Cheap beer and table football make this cosy little bar a must-visit for pub sports enthusiasts.

8 The Oak Room
MAP C3 ▪ Birkegade 10 ▪ 38 60 38 60 ▪ Open Wed–Sat ▪ www.oakroom.dk
This cocktail bar consists of one long narrow room, and offers balanced drinks, good music and great service. Popular with locals.

9 Mexibar
MAP C3 ▪ Elmegade 27 ▪ 35 37 77 66 ▪ Closed Sun
This cosy, Mexican-inspired bar serves good cocktails. The staff create a friendly atmosphere.

10 Rust
MAP C3 ▪ Guldbergsgade 8 ▪ 35 24 52 00 ▪ Open 11pm–4am Wed, 8pm–5am Fri & Sat ▪ www.rust.dk
Tune into Copenhagen's alternative live music scene at this bar (see p56), spread over three floors.

The bar and booths at Rust

Places to Eat

1 Orangeriet Kongens Have

MAP K3 ■ Kronprinsessegade 13 ■ 33 11 13 07 ■ Close Sun D ■ www.restaurant-orangeriet.dk ■ ⓚ ⓚ

This orangery in the park offers open sandwiches during the day and light seasonal dishes in the evening, in a dining room or on a large terrace.

Interior of Orangeriet Kongens Have

2 Ida Davidsen

MAP K3 ■ Store Kongensgade 70 ■ 33 91 36 55 ■ Open 10:30am–5pm, closed Sat–Sun & Jul ■ www.idadavidsen.dk ■ ⓚ

Excellent *smørrebrød* are on offer here, with an array of toppings.

3 Restaurant Zeleste

MAP L4 ■ Store Strandstræde 6 ■ 33 16 06 06 ■ Open 11:30am–8:30pm daily ■ www.zeleste.dk ■ ⓚ ⓚ

This restaurant with a cosy interior serves elegant Danish dishes.

4 Kiin Kiin

MAP C3 ■ Guldbergsgade 21 ■ 35 35 75 55 ■ Open 5:30pm–midnight Mon–Sat ■ www.kiin.dk ■ ⓚ ⓚ

Thai street food meets inventive fusion cooking at this restaurant *(see p60)*.

5 Bæst

MAP C3 ■ Guldbergsgade 29 ■ 35 35 04 63 ■ www.baest.dk ■ ⓚ ⓚ

This Italian inspired diner produces all charcuterie and cheeses in house and serves wood-fired pizzas.

6 Ramen To Biiru

MAP C3 ■ Griffenfeldsgade 28 ■ 50 53 02 22 ■ www.ramentobiiru.dk ■ ⓚ

This quirky craft beer and noodle bar oozes authenticity, right down to the retro-futuristic vending machine where you place your order.

7 Salt Bar and Restaurant

MAP L3 ■ Toldbodgade 24–8 ■ 33 74 14 44 ■ Open daily ■ www.saltrestaurant.dk ■ ⓚ ⓚ

In an airy 18th-century granary, this elegant bar and restaurant serves cocktails and innovative French-Danish cuisine.

8 Relæ

Jægersborggade ■ 36 96 66 09 ■ Open noon–1:30pm, 5pm–10pm daily (closed lunch Fri & Sat) ■ www.restaurant-relae.dk ■ ⓚ ⓚ ⓚ ⓚ

Savour New Nordic cuisine that is Michelin-starred yet budget-friendly, in a laid-back environment *(see p60)*.

9 Fischer

MAP E2 ■ Victor Borges Plads 12 ■ 35 42 39 64 ■ Open 5:30pm–midnight Wed–Sat ■ www.hosfischer.dk ■ ⓚ ⓚ

This tiny Italian restaurant is a favourite with local restaurant critics. Booking is essential.

10 Kate's Joint

MAP C4 ■ Blågårdsgade 12 ■ 35 37 44 96 ■ Open D only ■ ⓚ

At this place, on offer are cheap dishes with Malay, Middle Eastern and Indian influences.

See map on pp76–7

TOP 10 Vesterbro and Frederiksberg

Vesterbro and Frederiksberg lie side by side to the southwest and west of the Inner City. In the 19th century both areas were outside the city walls; this was when Tivoli was built on Vesterbro's edge. Vesterbro formerly included a red-light district, and its poor lived in humble flats with no running water. Although the area retains an edginess shared only by the Nørrebro district, much of it has now been regenerated. Today, you will find a thriving underground culture, restaurants and bars, designer outlets and a multicultural population. In contrast, prosperous Frederiksberg is still a tranquil, upmarket residential area.

Flying Toucan

VESTERBRO AND FREDERIKSBERG

Previous pages The chapel at Frederiksberg Slot

Tycho Brahe Planetarium exterior

1 Tycho Brahe Planetarium
MAP C5 ▪ Gammel Kongevej 10 ▪ Open noon–7:10pm Mon, 9:30am–7:10pm Tue–Sun ▪ Adm; free with Copenhagen Card ▪ www.tycho.dk

The permanent exhibition at the planetarium includes displays on the natural sciences, astronomy and space travel. However, one of the biggest attractions is the IMAX cinema: visitors are blown away by the high-quality images on the enormous 1,000-sq-m (10,760-sq-ft) dome screen. Films shown here cover topics such as astronomy and space research, and virtually transport you to another world. The minimum age for the film audience is 3 years.

2 Frederiksberg Slot
MAP A5 ▪ Roskildevej 28A ▪ 72 81 77 71

Set in Frederiksberg Have, one of the most romantic spots in Copenhagen, this Baroque-style palace was the royal family's summer residence until the mid-1800s. It's perched on a park hilltop, surrounded by many lovely little bridges, and the Chinese Pavilion that was erected in 1799 as a royal teahouse. It now houses the Danish Officer's Academy and is only open for guided tours.

3 Frederiksberg Have
MAP A5 ▪ Frederiksberg Runddel ▪ 33 95 42 00 ▪ Open 7am–sunset daily

Surrounding Frederiksberg Slot, this park is one of the city's loveliest green areas. Between 1798 and 1802, the original Baroque gardens were landscaped to conform with the Romantic style of the English garden. Several buildings here date to the Golden Age (1800–50), including the Chinese Pavilion and the Apis Temple.

Frederiksberg Have in the summer

- Top 10 Sights *see pp87–9*
- Places to Eat *see p91*
- Shopping *see p90*

4 Visit Carlsberg

MAP A6 ■ Gamle Carlsberg Vej 11 ■ 33 27 10 20 ■ Open 10am–5pm daily ■ Adm (free for under-6s); free with Copenhagen Card ■ www. visitcarlsberg.dk

A legendary landmark, this is the place where the famous brewery was founded back in 1847, growing beyond its local roots and transforming into a world-renowned power brand. A treat for all senses, this offers the smell of beer ingredients, the sight of outstanding architecture, songs of old brewers and of course a taste of the beer itself. Visitors can opt for a self-guided tour or take the help of the experienced guides, to know more about the place.

5 Zoologisk Have

MAP A5 ■ Roskildevej 32 ■ 72 20 02 00 ■ Open Apr–May & Sep: 10am–5pm Mon–Fri, 10am–6pm Sat–Sun; Jun & last 2 weeks of Aug: 10am–6pm daily; Jul & first 2 weeks of Aug: 10am–8pm daily; Oct– Mar: 10am–4pm daily (until 5pm Oct) ■ Adm; free with Copenhagen Card ■ www.zoo.dk

Open 365 days a year, this zoo makes for a lovely day out. Here you will find a wide variety of animals, from tigers to monkeys (including tiny, endangered Golden Lion Tamarins). Make sure you visit the Arctic Ring exhibit, which gives you a unique opportunity to get closer to the magnificent polar bears, North Atlantic birds and seals.

Interior of the Cisternerne

6 Cisternerne – The Cisterns

MAP A6 ■ Søndermarken ■ 33 21 93 10 ■ Open 11am–6pm daily (until 8pm Thu) ■ Closed Dec–Feb ■ Adm; free for under-18s ■ www.cisternerne.dk

Once the subterranean water reservoir of the city, this space is now famous for contemporary art exhibitions. The dimly lit 19th-century dripstone cave is immense, engulfing and slightly spooky; the art experience, though, is guaranteed to be magical.

7 Radisson Blu Royal Hotel

This 20-storey tower-block hotel, designed by architect Arne Jacobsen, represents the cutting-edge design style of the 1950s. The hotel *(see p116)* is littered with his iconic Egg and Swan chairs.

A tiger relaxes in the snow at Zoologisk Have

8 Sønder Boulevard
MAP C6

Following a transformation in 2007 which resulted in a long, green belt with endless possibilities for activities for all ages, Sønder Boulevard is regarded as one of Vesterbro's most popular recreational areas and hang-out spots. The area is filled with shops and great cafés. There are a few grounds, some with artificial grass for ball games and a field with asphalt for biking. The strip stretching from one end to the other composes a perfect spot for children to run around and play in.

9 Bakkehuset
MAP B6 ■ Rahbeks Allé 23, Frederiksberg ■ 33 31 43 62 ■ Open 11am–4pm Tue–Sun ■ Adm ■ www.bakkehusmuseet.dk

Formerly the home of 19th-century Golden Age literary personalities Knud Lyne and Kamma Rahbek, this old house is now a cultural museum.

A room at Bakkehuset

10 Storm P Museet
MAP A5 ■ Frederiksberg Runddel ■ 38 86 05 00 ■ Open 10am–4pm Tue–Sun ■ Adm; free with Copenhagen Card ■ www.stormp.dk

This small museum is a delightful find. It is dedicated to the whimsical and satirical wit of the Danish cartoonist Storm P, whose distinctive style seems to recall the social realism of the late 19th and early 20th centuries, such as the styles of Daumier and Degas. His great sense of humour comes through in the dialogues of his characters. If you speak Danish, you will derive great enjoyment from these cartoons.

A WALK AROUND VESTERBRO

▶ MORNING

Start at the city's **central station**, Hovedbanegård, and admire the **Frihedsstøtten** or "pillar of freedom" (1792). Continue down Vesterbrogade and take a left at Reventlowsgade, then take a right onto Istedgade. Walk up to **Halmtorvet**, a former cattle market now full of cafés, known as Den Brune Kødby ("brown meat city"). The building opposite is **Øksnehallen**, Vesterbro's biggest cultural exhibition space. Stroll to the blue-painted complex, **Den Hvide Kødby** ("white meat city"), now a lively cluster of bars and galleries. Head back to Halmtorvet, walk on and take a right on Skydebanegade. At the end of the street is a wall that protected inhabitants from shooting practice in the gardens on the other side. Enter the gate in the wall, turn left and walk through the park on your right to **Vesterbrogade**. Turn left and walk down the street, taking a left onto Oehlenschlægersgade, where you will find an extraordinary **mosaic-covered building** created by the late Nigerian-born artist Manuel Tafat.

AFTERNOON

Head back to Vesterbrogade for lunch at **Les Trois Cochons** *(see p91)*, or continue down Oehlenschlægersgade until you reach the trendy bars and boutiques on Istedgade. You could also stop for lunch or a drink at **Café Bang & Jensen** *(see p91)*. Spend the rest of the afternoon browsing in the stylish shops.

See map on pp86–7

Shopping

A coffee lounge on Værnedamsvej

1 Kyoto
MAP C6 ▪ Istedgade 95 ▪ 33
31 66 36 ▪ www.kyoto.dk

This store has fashionable wear from Scandinavian and French brands for both men and women, as well as a substantial collection of sneakers.

2 Donn Ya Doll
MAP C5 ▪ Istedgade 55 ▪ 33
22 66 35

Donn Ya Doll opened in the 1990s and has something of a space-age look. It stocks original accessories and clothing, some designed by the owner.

3 Girlie Hurly
MAP C6 ▪ Istedgade 99 ▪ 33
24 22 41

This shop is filled with quirky, colourful items for girls, from bags and candles to lamps and crockery.

4 Rockahula
MAP C6 ▪ Istedgade 91 ▪ www.
rockahula.dk

This intriguing little boutique is dedicated to all things 1950s and rockabilly, including a children's line.

5 Heidi & Bjarne
MAP C5 ▪ Istedgade 85
▪ www.heidiogbjarne.dk

A good place for stylish and casual children's clothes ranging from newborns to 12-year-olds. Proceeds are donated to Settlementet, a nonprofit.

6 Værnedamsvej
MAP C5

This gourmet food street has wine and chocolate shops, butchers and fishmongers among other stores.

7 Edison & Co.
MAP C6 ▪ Sønder Boulevard 39
▪ 61 67 26 94 ▪ www.edisonogco.dk

If you are looking for a souvenir to take back home, this store offers a variety of furniture and other decorative items for interiors.

8 Meyers Deli
MAP B5 ▪ Gammel Kongevej
107 ▪ 33 25 45 95 ▪ Open until 9pm
daily ▪ www.meyersdeli.dk

Claus Meyer helped kickstart the Nordic kitchen movement and his deli provides Noma-style food, from relishes to ready meals.

9 Dora
MAP C5 ▪ Værnedamsvej 6
▪ 32 21 33 57 ▪ www.shopdora.dk

Stylish and playful homewares, beautiful jewellery, fun stationery and more; all with reasonable price tags.

10 DANSK Made for Rooms
MAP C5 ▪ Istedgade 80 ▪ 32 18
02 55 ▪ www.danskmadeforrooms.dk

An enclave of slick Danish design, from prints and kitchen appliances to decor. Great for window-shopping on Vesterbo's vibrant high street.

Places to Eat

PRICE CATEGORIES

For a three-course meal for one without alcohol, including taxes and charges.

Ⓚ under 300 Dkr ⓀⓀ 300–500 Dkr
ⓀⓀⓀ over 500 Dkr

1 Gorilla

MAP D6 ▪ Flæsketorvet 63
▪ 33 33 83 30 ▪ Open 5:30pm–midnight Mon–Thu; 5:30pm–2am Fri & Sat
▪ www.restaurantgorilla.dk ▪ ⓀⓀ

Tuck into shared plates of organic, sumptuous Scandi-tapas while slurping biodynamic wines at this trendy brasserie-style restaurant in Kødbyen.

2 Sticks 'n' Sushi

MAP C6 ▪ Istedgade 62
▪ 33 23 73 04 ▪ www.sushi.dk ▪ Ⓚ Ⓚ

Try mouthwatering sushi, sashimi or yakitori at this Euro-Japanese café-bar.

Sushi plate at Sticks 'n' Sushi

3 Kul

MAP C5 ▪ Høkerboderne 16b
▪ 33 21 00 33 ▪ Open 5pm–11pm Sun–Wed (till 11:30pm Thu, 1am Fri–Sat) ▪ www.restaurantkul.dk ▪ ⓀⓀ

This uber-hip restaurant (see p61) in the meatpacking district has its own custom-built grill and a knack for pulling off unlikely food pairings.

4 Cofoco

MAP C5 ▪ Abel Cathrines Gade 7 ▪ 33 13 60 60 ▪ Book ahead ▪ Ⓚ

Delicious and reasonably priced Mediterranean-Danish food is served at a long communal table.

5 Café Bang & Jensen

MAP C6 ▪ Istedgade 130
▪ 33 25 53 18 ▪ www.bangogjensen.dk ▪ Ⓚ

This former pharmacy is now a popular café-bar. Fun cocktails and good music make for lively nights.

6 Famo

MAP C5 ▪ Saxogade 3 ▪ 33 23 22 50 ▪ www.famo.dk ▪ ⓀⓀ

Locals head here for good-quality, inexpensive Italian cuisine.

7 Frederiks Have

MAP A4 ▪ Smallegade 41 ▪ 38 88 33 35 ▪ Closed Sun ▪ www.frederikshave.dk ▪ ⓀⓀ

Housed in a 19th-century building, Frederiks Have serves Swedish and Danish specialities.

8 Mother

MAP C6 ▪ Høkerboderne 9–15 ▪ 22 27 58 98 ▪ www.mother.dk ▪ Ⓚ

This pizzeria is known for organic sourdough bases and fresh, classic toppings.

9 Formel B

MAP B5 ▪ Vesterbrogade 182 ▪ 33 25 10 66 ▪ Closed Sun ▪ www.formelb.dk ▪ ⓀⓀⓀ

Enjoy delicate small plates made with farm-fresh ingredients. Known for a selection of natural wines (see p60).

10 Les Trois Cochons

MAP C5 ▪ Værnedamsvej 10
▪ 33 31 70 55 ▪ Ⓚ

Aptly named ("the three pigs" in French), this restaurant serves great southern French food, all day long.

Dining booths at Les Trois Cochons

See map on pp86–7

🔟 Christianshavn and Holmen

After the Inner City, this settlement on the island of Amager is the oldest part of Copenhagen. In 1521, Christian II invited Dutch gardeners (whom he held in high regard) to this fertile area to plant and run market gardens. A century later, Christian IV built fortifications in the area and a town on an island at the north end. The canals of Christianshavn, lined with houseboats and pretty 17th-century houses, are a charming attraction. Holmen to the north consists of three man-made islets and was created in 1690 as a naval base. After the navy left in the late 20th century, the area saw an increase in public spaces, housing and art and design schools; it is also home to the city's impressive Opera House.

CHRISTIANSHAVN AND HOLMEN

Inderhavnsbroen bridge

1 Christians Kirke

MAP K6 ■ Strandgade 1 ■ 32
54 15 76 ■ Open 10am–4pm Tue–Fri
■ www.christianskirke.com

Originally known as Frederiks Kirke,
this yellow-brick church was renamed
Christians Kirke (after Christian IV,
founder of this part of Copenhagen) in
1901. It was built between 1755 and
1759 in the Rococo style by Nicolai
Eigtved, Frederik V's master architect.
The interior resembles a theatre, with
second-level seating galleries and the
altar taking the place of the stage.
The elegant tower was added by
Eigtved's son-in-law, G D Anthon,
10 years after the church was built.

2 Inderhavnen

MAP J6–M4

Christianshavn is dominated by
waterways. Its canals are tributaries
of the Inner Harbour (Inderhavnen),
which separates it from the rest of the
city, eventually widening to become
the Øresund (Sound). A harbour tour
is a great way to
appreciate the area.

**Sailing boats at
Gammel Dok**

3 Harbour Circle

MAP K6–L5

Completed in 2017, the Harbour
Circle route is part of Copenhagen's
push for sustainable urban transport. The scenic pedestrian and
cyclist path connects previously
disjointed neighbourhoods along
the city harbour, from Holmen and
Nyhavn in the north to Christianshavn
and southernmost Slusen. The route
is connected by architecturally
noteworthy bridges. Inderhavnsbroen
(built 2016), nicknamed "The Kissing
Bridge", connects Nyhavn and the
city centre with Christianshavn and
Holmen. Platforms on the bridge
offer spectacular views of the harbour
area. Danish-Icelandic architect
Olafur Eliasson designed the striking
Cirkelbroen (The Circle Bridge): five
touching circular platforms with ship
masts link central Christianshavn to
Appelbys Plads.

4 Gammel Dok

MAP L5 ■ National Workshops
for Art, Strandgade 27B ■ 32 96 05 10

Gammel Dok ("Old Dock") was built
in 1739, a time when the navy's ships
moored in the local area. Denmark's
first dry dock, it was located at this
site till 1919. The warehouse dates
back to 1882 and the building was
acquired by the Danish state in 1979,
when it was restored. It now serves
as a popular historical site, and is also
home to the National Workshops for
Art. Artists, designers and restorers
can apply for a residency to practise
their craft here.

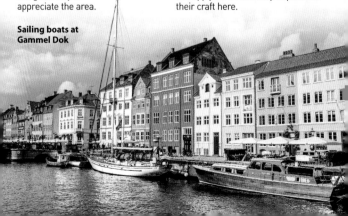

⑤ Holmen and Refshaleøen

MAP M4

North of Christianshavn are Holmen and Refshaleøen, a former shipyard that is home to various sporting activities and is now a major dining destination. Innovative restaurants here include Noma (see p97), and you will also find a new version of the Copenhagen Street Food Market.

North Atlantic House, a former warehouse

⑥ Vor Frelsers Kirke

MAP L6 ■ Sankt Annae Gade 29 ■ 32 54 68 83 ■ Church: Open 11am–3:30pm daily ■ Tower: Open Mar–Apr & Oct–Nov: 10am–4pm Mon–Sat, 10:30am–4pm Sun; May–Sep: 9:30am–7pm Mon–Sat, 10:30am–7pm Sun ■ Adm for tower; free with Copenhagen Card ■ www.vorfrelserskirke.dk

This magnificent Baroque church was built in 1682–96 by the Dutch-Norwegian architect Lambert van Haven in the form of a Greek cross. Its trademark twisted tower was added 50 years later. Inside the church, keep an eye out for the putti-covered font, presented in 1702 by Frederik IV's morganatic wife. The altarpiece is a must-see – it represents God as the Sun and depicts the scene in the garden of Gethsemane.

⑦ North Atlantic House

MAP M4 ■ Strandgade 91 ■ 32 83 37 00 ■ Open 10am–5pm Mon–Fri, noon–5pm Sat & Sun ■ Adm; free for under-11s and with Copenhagen Card ■ www.nordatlantens.dk

The North Atlantic House is a cultural centre for Greenland, Iceland and the Faroes. It is housed in an 18th-century warehouse, formerly the Greenlandic Trading Square, which hosts art displays and events.

⑧ Overgaden Neden Vandet and Overgaden Oven Vandet

MAP L6–M5

These two cobbled streets lie on either side of the Christianshavns canal. Overgaden Neden Vandet ("upper street below the water") is the quayside that runs along the Sound side of the canal. It is lined with 17th-century buildings, one of which is the Era Ora restaurant (see p97). Overgaden Oven Vandet ("upper street above the water") is also lined with 17th-century houses.

⑨ Operaen

MAP M3 ■ Ekvipagemestervej 10 ■ 33 69 69 69 ■ Guided tours available ■ www.kglteater.dk

Completed in 2004, the Opera House was the first major public building to be built in the Holmen area after the navy vacated the docks. Architect Henning Larsen emphasized its location near the water, creating a

The twisted tower of Vor Frelsers Kirke

building with large glass windows and no pillars on the ground floor so as not to obstruct the view. The interior was designed to have a maritime feel as well, with big balconies, open spaces and white railings. The position of the Opera House caused major controversy when it was built, as it lies directly opposite Amalienborg. The design of the Opera House was also the cause of some friction when its benefactor, Mærsk McKinney Møller, insisted that his own ideas be incorporated into the construction. It is one of the most expensive opera houses ever built, thanks to its marble foyer and gold-leaf auditorium ceiling.

Modern interior of Operaen

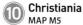
⑩ Christiania
MAP M5

This rebellious squatters' enclave (see pp28–9), set up in the 1970s in abandoned military barracks, was an inspirational new society with its own set of laws, readily available drugs and no tax system. The area has now become a bit more conventional; the inhabitants have been paying taxes since 1994. In 2011, residents and the state came to an agreement giving Christiania residents the right to buy, making the squat official for the first time. There are no actual sights but many hippy hangouts.

A WALKING TOUR OF THE AREA

▶ MORNING

Start at the Knippelsbro bridge. Built in 1937, the bridge takes its name from Hans Knip, the tollkeeper. Turn right to visit **Christians Kirke** (see p41) on Strandgade. Head north on Johan Semps Gade to catch a glimpse of **Den Sorte Diamant** library (see p12) across the harbour, then head west to cross **Cirkelbroen** (see p93), a pedestrian and bike bridge. Follow the path past Appelbys Plads to **Overgaden Oven Vandet**. Take a left and walk along the canal. Stop at No. 32 (built 1622–4), on Strandgade, which is said to be the oldest house in Christianshavn. From here, turn right onto Sankt Annæ Gade to see **Vor Frelsers Kirke**. If you are curious about **Christiania**, follow Overgaden Oven Vandet until you can take a right down Brobergsgade, passing through the gate reading "You are now leaving the EU." Alternatively, stroll canalside and go right at Bodenhoffs Plads, then head left onto Værftsbroen. Keep walking towards the **Opera House**. Hop on a harbour bus back to Knippelsbro for lunch at **Café Wilder** (see p97) on Wildersgade.

AFTERNOON

Spend the afternoon doing some leisurely shopping. If you are in the mood for a drink, there are a number of cafés all along the Christianshavns Kanal. Linger over supper at **Restaurant Barr** (Strandgade; tel: 32 96 32 93) or catch a performance at the **Opera House** (taking bus No. 9A or the harbour bus from Knippelsbro).

See map on p92

Shopping

1 Bit Antik
MAP L6 ■ Prinsessegade 17B
■ 40 72 09 62 ■ Open 3–6pm Wed
■ www.bitantik.dk

This tiny shop is filled with pieces from Denmark's yesteryears, including old dolls and doll houses, books, glasses, sculpture and porcelain objects.

2 Aurum
MAP L6
■ Dronningensgade 23
■ 25 30 00 11 ■ www.
aurumcph.com

Some 20 international jewellers, including Marco Vallejo, are represented at Aurum. Many materials, including precious stones, are used to create these unique pieces.

Gold ring by Marco Vallejo

3 Porte à Gauche
MAP L5 ■ Torvegade 20 ■ 32 54 01 40 ■ www.porteagauche.dk

This trendy boutique offers chic, minimalist Scandinavian designer wear for women. You will also find a classic, exotic collection of Julie Sandlau jewellery.

4 Mo Christianshavn
MAP L5 ■ Torvegade 24
■ 26 80 17 26 ■ Open Tue–Sat
■ www.mo.dk

This small shop and workshop is owned by Mo, a popular local jewellery designer.

5 Ganni Postmodern
MAP L6 ■ Overgaden Oven Vandet 40 ■ 28 35 55 56 ■ www.ganni.com

This is the first Ganni Postmodern concept store in the city. The headquarters are also in Copenhagen, and there are stores across the world.

6 Lagkagehuset
MAP L6 ■ Torvegade 45
■ 32 57 36 07 ■ Open from 6am daily

Well known for its breads, cakes and pastries, this bakery has a fine selection during Christmas.

7 Kvindesmedien
MAP M5 ■ Mælkevejen 83
■ 32 57 76 58

This artistic workshop offers high quality steel design. For one of a kind decorations and sculptures, this is the place to go.

8 Hilbert København
MAP L6 ■ Sankt Annæ Gade 24 ■ 33 93 53 01
■ Closed Sat

Jewellery is made to order here by goldsmith Morten Hilbert.

9 Cibi e Vini
MAP L5 ■ Torvegade 28
■ 32 57 77 98 ■ www.cibievini.dk

This Italian delicatessen sells wine, bread, pasta and meats.

10 Christiania Shop
MAP M5 ■ Loppebygningen
■ 60 80 88 62

Located in the same building as the Christiania art gallery, this shop sells many Christiania souvenirs.

Mannequins outside Christiania Shop

Places to Eat

PRICE CATEGORIES
For a three-course meal for one without alcohol, including taxes and charges.

Ⓚ under 300 Dkr Ⓚ Ⓚ 300–500 Dkr
Ⓚ Ⓚ Ⓚ over 500 Dkr

1 Era Ora
MAP L6 ▪ Overgaden Neden Vandet 33B ▪ 32 54 06 93 ▪ Closed Sun ▪ www.era-ora.dk ▪ Ⓚ Ⓚ Ⓚ

One of the best Italian restaurants in Denmark, Era Ora *(see p60)* offers warm service in a tranquil setting, delicious food and a vast wine list. Book ahead.

2 Kadeau
MAP L6 ▪ Wildersgade 10B ▪ 33 25 22 23 ▪ Closed Sun–Tue, L ▪ www.kadeau.dk ▪ Ⓚ Ⓚ Ⓚ

The menu at this Michelin-starred New Nordic restaurant *(see p60)* is like a love letter to the island of Bornholm, from where all the seasonal ingredients are painstakingly sourced.

3 Noma
Refshalevej 96 ▪ 32 96 32 97 ▪ Closed Sun–Tue ▪ www.noma.dk ▪ Ⓚ Ⓚ Ⓚ

Copenhagen's ultimate Michelin-star restaurant reopened on Refshaleøen in 2018. The restaurant serves a New Nordic tasting menu from three seasonal themes: seafood, vegetables, and game and forest. Book ahead.

4 Luna's Diner
MAP L5 ▪ Sankt Annæ Gade 5 ▪ 32 54 20 00 ▪ www.lunasdiner.dk ▪ Ⓚ Ⓚ

Popular American-style diner in the heart of Christianshaven known for its burgers, breakfasts and vegetarian options.

5 Café Wilder
MAP L5 ▪ Wildersgade 56 ▪ 32 54 71 83 ▪ www.cafewilder.dk ▪ Ⓚ Ⓚ

Locals and tourists come here to enjoy good French- and Italian-inspired food and coffee.

6 Sofiekælderen
MAP L6 ▪ Overgaden Oven Vandet 32 ▪ 32 57 77 01 ▪ Closed Sun ▪ www.sofiekaelderen.dk ▪ Ⓚ Ⓚ Ⓚ

This café-bar is so close to the water, you could climb down to the boats moored alongside.

7 108
MAP M4 ▪ Strandgade 108 ▪ 32 96 32 92 ▪ www.108.dk ▪ Ⓚ Ⓚ Ⓚ

The sister to Noma, this harbourside bistro offers a masterclass in New Nordic cooking – and a fascinating selection of biodynamic wines.

Chic dining setting at 108

8 Rabes Have
MAP K6 ▪ Langebrogade 8 ▪ 32 57 34 17 ▪ Open until 5pm ▪ Closed Mon–Tue ▪ Ⓚ

Opened for soldiers and sailors in 1632, this is the oldest pub in the city.

9 Parterre
MAP M5 ▪ Overgaden Oven Vandet 90 ▪ Ⓚ

A gorgeous, hidden-gem basement café on Christianshaven's canal, quite popular for breakfast and lunch.

10 Oven Vande Café
MAP L5 ▪ Overgaden Oven Vandet 44 ▪ 32 95 96 02 ▪ www.cafeovenvande.dk ▪ Ⓚ Ⓚ

Enjoy tasty salads, soups and paninis at this café with outdoor seating.

See map on p92

TOP 10 Beyond Copenhagen

Although Copenhagen itself will easily keep you entertained for days, the area around the city offers many excursion options. Roskilde and Helsingør provide a taste of Nordic history, from the Viking era to the founding of Copenhagen. Get a sense of medieval maritime defence of the Sound at Helsingør's Kronborg Slot or explore royal lifestyles of the 17th and 18th centuries at Frederiksborg and Charlottenlund. Art- and literature-lovers will enjoy Arken, Louisiana, Ordrupgaard and the Karen Blixen Museet. Frilandsmuseet and Den Blå Planet are must-visits for kids.

Windmill at Frilandsmuseet

BEYOND COPENHAGEN

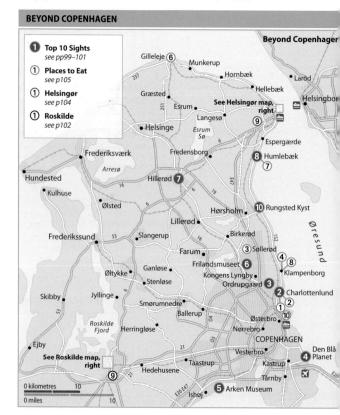

- **1** Top 10 Sights
  see pp99–101
- ① Places to Eat
  see p105
- ① Helsingør
  see p104
- ① Roskilde
  see p102

Replica Viking longboats on the water in Roskilde

1 Roskilde

The town of Roskilde makes for a fascinating day out. You will find a medieval cathedral, a royal burial site and the wonderful Viking Ship Museum *(see p102)*, which offers fjord trips on replica Viking longboats.

2 Charlottenlund Slotshave

MAP B2 ▪ Open Mon–Fri
▪ www.slke.dk

The park around Charlottenlund Slot is a 16-minute train ride from the city centre. Redesigned in the Romantic English style in the 19th century, the park includes a charming thatched cottage, once lodgings for the Royal Life Guards. The palace itself is closed to the public.

3 Ordrupgaard

MAP B2 ▪ Vilvordevej 110, Charlottenlund ▪ 39 64 11 83 ▪ Gallery open: 1–5pm Tue–Fri; Finn Juhl's House: 11am–4:45pm Sat, Sun & public holidays ▪ Adm; free for under-18s; free with Copenhagen Card
▪ Free audio guide; book for English guided tours ▪ www.ordrupgaard.dk

This gallery has a collection of French Impressionist art and works by 19th- and 20th-century Danish artists. The 19th-century mansion has a modern extension by the late architect Zaha Hadid. Within the same complex is furniture designer Finn Juhl's house, now a gallery exhibiting his work.

The interior of Finn Juhl's house

Marine life at Den Blå Planet

exhibitions. The white, ship-like museum building, designed by Danish architect Søren Lund, could be an exhibit in itself. It offers great views of the sea at Køge Bugt.

4 Den Blå Planet

MAP C3 ■ Jacob Fortlingsvej 1, Kastrup ■ 44 22 22 44 ■ Open 10am–5pm daily (until 9pm Mon) ■ Adm; free with Copenhagen Card ■ www.denblaaplanet.dk

Denmark's national aquarium Den Blå Planet is famous for its architecture inspired by the currents of a whirlpool (the lobby is akin to a vortex). With 53 aquariums and installations, it is said to be the most modern aquarium in Northern Europe.

5 Arken Museum for Moderne Kunst

MAP B3 ■ Skovvej 100, Ishøj ■ 43 54 02 22 ■ Open 10am–9pm Tue–Thu (until 5pm Fri–Sun) ■ Adm; free with Copenhagen Card ■ www.arken.dk

This wonderful museum houses a rotating permanent collection of contemporary international and Danish art, along with temporary

6 Frilandsmuseet

MAP B2 ■ Konggevejen 100, Kongens Lyngby ■ 41 20 64 55 ■ Open May–mid-Oct: 10am–4pm Tue–Sun (Jul & first 2 wks of Aug: until 5pm) ■ en.natmus.dk

Part of the Nationalmuseet (see pp32–3), Denmark's Open Air Museum brings history alive through working exhibits from the period 1650–1940. Explore farms, windmills and a cooperative village. There are old Danish breeds of livestock, including pigs, sheep and geese.

7 Frederiksborg Slot

MAP B2 ■ DK-3400 Hillerød ■ 48 26 04 39 ■ Museum: open Apr–Oct: 10am–5pm daily; Nov–Mar: 11am–3pm ■ Baroque gardens: open 10am–sundown daily ■ Adm (museum only) ■ www.dnm.dk

This copper-turreted castle (see p42) is situated on three islets in a lake that is surrounded by Baroque gardens. It was built in 1602–20 for Christian IV. The interior is a mix of Renaissance and Baroque decor. After a fire in 1859, the castle was rescued from ruin by J C Jacobsen (of Carlsberg fame), who founded a museum here.

The Great Hall at Frederiksborg Slot

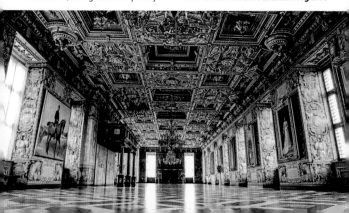

8 Louisiana Museum

MAP B1 ■ Gammel Strandvej 13, Humlebæk ■ 49 19 07 19 ■ Open 11am–10pm Tue–Fri, 11am–6pm Sat & Sun ■ Adm for adults; free with Copenhagen Card ■ English guided tours available ■ www.louisiana.dk

This museum (see p103) houses an impressive selection of works by international artists like Picasso and Francis Bacon, and Danish masters including Asger Jorn and Per Kirkeby. There is also a children's wing, which offers art-related activities for kids aged between 3 and 16 years. The coastal location, sculpture park and excellent café make the museum even more appealing for visitors.

Courtyard at Kronborg Slot

9 Helsingør

In the 1400s, this harbour town (see p104) levied tax on all sea traffic that passed through the Sound. A pretty medieval centre aside, there is the 16th-century castle, Kronborg Slot, the Carmelite monastery and the Maritime Museum of Denmark.

10 Karen Blixen Museet

MAP B2 ■ Rungsted Strandvej 111, Rungsted Kyst ■ 45 57 10 57 ■ Open May–Sep: 10am–5pm Tue–Sun; Oct–Apr: 1–4pm Wed–Fri, 11am–4pm Sat & Sun ■ Adm; free for under-14s; free with Copenhagen Card ■ Book ahead for guided tours in English ■ www.blixen.dk

Karen Blixen (pen name: Isak Dinesen), the author of the acclaimed memoir *Out of Africa*, was born here in 1885. Blixen returned in 1931 and the house is exactly as it was when she lived here.

DAY TOUR BEYOND COPENHAGEN

▶ MORNING

From Københavns Hovedbanegård (Copenhagen Central Station), take a train and head to the town of **Helsingør** to explore the local museums and castles. Have a wander around **Kronborg Slot** (see p104), a lovely 16th- century castle with a banqueting hall, royal chambers and casemates, and see why it was immortalized as Elsinore in Hamlet. After your castle tour, stop by the **Maritime Museum of Denmark** (see p104). For lunch, return to the town square and sit down for an open sandwich and a beer at one of its numerous pubs. After lunch, wander through the medieval streets, especially Stendgade and Strandgade (see p104). Visit the medieval **Domkirke** and the **Bymuseum** (see p104), housed in a small Carmelite hospital dating back to 1520.

AFTERNOON

Take the train to Humlebæk and visit the **Louisiana Museum** (see p103), which stays open until 10pm on Tuesdays to Fridays. There are plenty of things to see here, and you can book into a guided tour that encompasses the museum's architecture and landscape. Then return to the station and take a train to Rungsted Kyst and drop in at the Karen Blixen Museet. After a walk around the house, garden and bird sanctuary, have coffee and one of the home-made cakes at the museum café. Head back towards Copenhagen in the early evening, stopping off en route at Klampenborg for dinner and an evening of entertainment at the **Bakken** funfair (see p52).

See map on p98 ←

Roskilde

1 Roskilde Domkirke
MAP P6 ▪ Domkirkestræde 10 ▪ 46 35 16 24 ▪ Opening hours vary; check website ▪ Adm; free with Copenhagen Card ▪ www.roskilde-domkirke.dk

This UNESCO World Heritage Site has the remains of 39 Danish monarchs.

Replica Viking vessels

2 Vikingeskibsmuseet
MAP P4 ▪ Vindeboder 12 ▪ 46 30 02 00 ▪ Open 10am–4pm daily (to 5pm Jul–Aug) ▪ Adm; free for under-18s ▪ www.vikingeskibsmuseet.dk

The popular Viking Ship Museum displays five 1,000-year-old Viking vessels. Boat trips available May–Sep.

3 Roskilde Museum
MAP P5 ▪ Sankt Ols Stræde 3 ▪ 46 31 65 00 ▪ Open 10am–4pm daily (until 9pm Wed) ▪ Adm; free with Copenhagen Card ▪ www.roskildemuseum.dk

This museum illustrates Roskilde's history from the time when it was Denmark's first capital.

4 Roskilde Kloster
MAP P6 ▪ Sankt Peders Straede 8E ▪ 46 35 02 19 ▪ www.roskildekloster.dk

This former convent was Denmark's first refuge for unmarried mothers.

5 Skomagergade and Algade
MAP P6

The city's two main cobbled streets are lined with shops and cafés.

6 Hestetorvet
MAP Q6

The Horse Market Place is set in what was Roskilde's largest square for centuries. Three giant vases here were created by artist Peter Brandes.

7 Kirkegård
MAP Q6

Now a park, this former medieval churchyard holds the graves of many prominent Roskilde citizens.

8 Stændertorvet
MAP P6 ▪ Markets on Wed & Sat

The city's central square in front of the Town Hall has been a market-place since the Middle Ages.

9 RAGNAROCK
Rabalderstræde 16 ▪ 46 31 68 54 ▪ Open 10am–5pm Tue, Thu–Sun (until 10pm Wed); closed Mon ▪ www.ragnarock.dk

This museum of pop, rock and youth culture offers a kaleidoscopic journey that aims to engage, educate, and inspire visitors.

10 Roskilde Palace
MAP P6 ▪ Stændertorvet 3D ▪ 46 31 65 70 ▪ Open noon–5pm Tue, Thu & Fri (until 8pm Wed), 11am–4pm Sat & Sun ▪ Adm for adults ▪ www.samtidskunst.dk

Built in 1733–6 for royal visitors, this yellow, four-wing Baroque building houses the country's first Museum of Contemporary Art.

Roskilde Palace

Louisiana Museum

Relaxing in the gardens of Louisiana Museum

1 Big Thumb (1968)
This striking, 2-m- (6-ft-) tall bronze thumb is modelled after the thumb of its creator, French sculptor César Baldaccini (1921–98).

2 Dead Drunk Danes (1960)
The Guggenheim International Award was given to rebel artist Asger Jorn (1914–73) for this abstract painting. However, he rejected the accolade and sent Harry Guggenheim an infuriated telegram: "Go to hell with your money bastard *stop* Never asked for it *stop* Against all decency to mix artist against his will in your publicity *stop*".

3 3 Gleaming Lights of the Souls (2008)
Japanese artist Yayoi Kusama's lyrical installation has mirrors and 100 lamps resembling glowing ping pong balls.

4 House to Watch the Sunset (2015)
Swiss artist Not Vital's house of steel blends in with its surroundings as it reflects the nature and changing seasons of the Sculpture Park in its shiny surface.

5 Little Janey Waney (1964/76)
This mobile installation by American artist Alexander Calder is a colourful sight, moving elegantly whenever the wind blows.

6 Alberto Giacometti Collection
The museum owns an impressive collection of 13 sculptures and several drawings by Giacometti (1901–66). The elongated figures with rough textures are reminiscent of African sculpture.

7 Two Piece Reclining Figure No 5 (1963–4)
This bronze work by Henry Moore (1898–1986) occupies a beautiful spot between the trees, its human-oid, organic forms melding with the landscape.

8 The Louisiana Butik
The museum shop carries a variety of high-quality Scandinavian design products, art and culture books and exhibition posters.

9 The Louisiana Cafe
The museum café has one of Denmark's most beautiful panoramic views over the Øresund to the coast of Sweden. The kitchen here serves contemporary Danish cuisine made with fresh seasonal produce.

10 The Sculpture Park
In the museum's sculpture park dotted by around 60 sculptures, the visual arts, architecture and landscapes exist in unity. The views are as much a part of the park's charm as its exhibits.

See map on p98

Helsingør

1 Maritime Museum of Denmark

MAP Q2 ■ Ny Kronborgvej 1 ■ 49 21 06 85 ■ Open Sep–Jun: 11am–5pm Tue–Sun; Jul–Aug: 10am–5pm daily ■ Adm; free with Copenhagen Card & for under-18s ■ www.mfs.dk

This interactive museum features hands-on digital exhibits.

2 Festivals

www.visitnordsjaelland.com

Helsingør's summer festivals include the CLICK festival (May), PASSAGE street theater festival (July) and the Shakespeare festival (August).

3 Karmeliterklosteret

MAP P2 ■ Sankt Anna Gade 38 ■ 49 21 17 74 ■ Open 10am–2pm Tue–Sun ■ Adm ■ www.sctmariae.dk

The Carmelite Order owned this 15th-century Gothic-style monastery.

4 Helsingør Bymuseum

MAP P2 ■ Sankt Anna Gade 36 ■ 49 28 18 00 ■ Open noon–4pm Tue–Fri & Sun, 10am–2pm Sat ■ Adm; free with Copenhagen Card ■ www. helsingormuseer.dk

Once a sailors' hospital, its exhibits recall its history and that of this medieval town.

5 Kronborg Slot

MAP Q2 ■ Kronborg 2C ■ 49 21 30 78 ■ Open 11am–4pm daily (Nov–Mar: closed Mon); Jun–Aug: 10am–5:30pm daily ■ Adm; free with Copenhagen Card ■ www.kongeligeslotte.dk

Known as the setting of Shakespeare's *Hamlet*, this castle *(see p42)* was built in 1420. The Great Hall here is the largest in Europe.

6 Culture Yard

MAP P3 ■ Havnepladsen 1 ■ 49 28 37 47 ■ Open 10am–9pm Mon–Fri, 10am–4pm Sat & Sun ■ www.kuto.dk

This cultural house has a multimedia library, cultural activities, and a café overlooking Kronborg Slot.

7 Stengade and Strandgade

MAP P3 ■ www.helsingormuseer.dk

Stengade is a pedestrianized street in the medieval quarter. Some houses on the parallel Strandgade date back to the 1400s.

8 Sankt Olai Kirke (Helsingør Domkirke)

MAP P2 ■ Sankt Anna Gade 12 ■ 49 21 04 43 ■ Open May–Aug: 10am–4pm Mon–Fri; Sep–Apr: 10am–2pm) ■ www.helsingoerdomkirke.dk

Note the 15th-century crucifix, 1568 Renaissance pulpit, 1579 baptismal font and carved wooden altar.

9 Danmarks Teknisk Museum

Fabriksvej 25 ■ 49 22 26 11 ■ Open Feb–Oct: 10am–5pm Tue–Sun (Nov–Jan: to 4pm) ■ Adm for adults ■ www.tekniskmuseum.dk

The machines at this museum of science and technology include steam engines, cars and aeroplanes.

10 Øresundsakvariet

MAP P1 ■ Strandpromenaden 5 ■ 35 32 19 70 ■ Open Jun–Aug: 10am–5pm daily; Sep–May: 10am–4pm Mon–Fri, 10am–5pm Sat & Sun ■ Adm; free with Copenhagen Card ■ www.oresundsakvariet.ku.dk

This small aquarium has a variety of tropical fish and Baltic species.

A yacht sailing past Kronborg Slot

Places to Eat

PRICE CATEGORIES

For a three-course meal for one without
alcohol, including taxes and charges.
....
Ⓚ under 300 Dkr ⓀⓀ 300–500 Dkr
ⓀⓀⓀ over 500 Dkr

① Café Bomhuset
MAP B2 ▪ Skovriderkroen,
Strandvejen 235, Charlottenlund
▪ 39 65 67 00 ▪ www.cafebomhuset.
dk ▪ ⒦Ⓚ

An upscale alternative to the typical
outdoor café. The terrace is popular.

② Café Jorden Rundt
MAP B2 ▪ Strandvejen
152, Charlottenlund
▪ 39 63 73 81 ▪ Ⓚ

This café offers great
sea views from its
panoramic windows.
Popular for brunch,
sandwiches and cakes.

③ Søllerød Kro
MAP B2
▪ Søllerødveg 35, Holte
▪ 45 80 25 05 ▪ Closed
Mon–Tue ▪ www.soelleroed-kro.dk
▪ ⓀⓀⓀ

This Michelin-starred restaurant has
set menus and à la carte dishes.

④ Den Gule Cottage
MAP B2 ▪ Taarbæk Strandvej 2,
Klampenborg ▪ 39 64 06 91 ▪ Closed
mid-Feb–May & mid-Nov–mid-Dec:
Mon–Wed; mid-Dec–mid-Feb ▪ www.
dengulecottage.dk ▪ ⒦Ⓚ

This cottage was designed in 1844 by
the great Danish architect Gottlieb
Bindesbøll. Dishes are prepared with
seasonal ingredients.

⑤ Mumm
MAP N6 ▪ Karen Olsdatters
Stræde 9, Roskilde ▪ 46 37 22 01
▪ Dinner only; closed Sun ▪ ⓀⓀⓀ

On one of Roskilde's oldest streets,
this upscale, tiny French-Danish
restaurant has a pretty courtyard.

⑥ Restaurant Gilleleje Havn
MAP A1 ▪ Havnevej 14,
Gilleleje ▪ 48 30 30 39 ▪ Closed Mon–
Tue ▪ www.gillelejehavn.dk ▪ ⒦Ⓚ

Enjoy traditional Danish seafood
at this old seamen's inn (1895).

⑦ Restaurant Sletten
MAP B2 ▪ Gl. Strandvej 137,
Humlebæk ▪ 49 19 13 21 ▪ Closed
Sep–May: Sun–Mon ▪ www.sletten.dk
▪ ⓀⓀⓀ

Sletten serves excellent value French
cuisine, with the bonus of a sea view.

The stylish interior of Den Røde Cottage

⑧ Den Røde Cottage
MAP B2 ▪ Strandvejen 550,
Klampenborg ▪ 31 90 46 14 ▪ D only;
closed Feb; Oct–Apr: Sun ▪ www.
denroedecottage.dk ▪ ⓀⓀⓀ

The sophisticated sister to Den Gule
Cottage next door, Den Røde offers
exquisite seasonal menus.

⑨ Snekken
MAP P4 ▪ Vindeboder 16,
Roskilde ▪ 46 35 98 16 ▪ www.
snekken.dk ▪ ⒦Ⓚ

Locals book a table at Snekken for
contemporary cuisine and sea views.

⑩ Paustian
MAP B2 ▪ Kalkbrænderiløbskaj
2, Copenhagen ▪ 39 18 55 01 ▪ www.
paustian.com ▪ ⒦Ⓚ

Attached to Paustian furniture house,
the interiors here are unsurprisingly
stunning. Gorgeous harbour views.

See map on p98–9

Streetsmart

Bicycles lined up outside a timber
framed building in the old town

Getting To and Around Copenhagen

Arriving by Air

Airlines flying directly to **Copenhagen Airport** include **Scandinavian Airlines**, **British Airways**, **easyJet** and **Norwegian**. The airport is located in Kastrup, 12 km (7 miles) southeast of the city. It takes around 15 minutes to reach the city centre by train or Metro (the station is near Terminal 3), or 45 minutes by bus (both cost the same). You will also find a taxi rank just outside Terminal 3. Expect to pay around 300 Dkr for a cab to the city centre.

Arriving by Train

Copenhagen is connected by train to many European cities, including Hamburg, Berlin and Stockholm. All international trains stop at the large Københavns Hovedbanegård central station, part of **Danish State Railways** (DSB). If you plan to travel on to Sweden, remember to bring your passport with you as there could be a border check at the first train stop in Sweden.

Arriving by Road

If you are driving to Copenhagen from Sweden, you can take the **Øresund Bridge** from Malmö. In case you are driving in from Germany and crossing the island of Funen, you can cross the **Great Belt Bridge** to Sjælland, the island on which the city of Copenhagen lies. Both bridges exact a toll.

Arriving by Ferry

You can take a **Polferries** ferry from Swinoujscie in Poland, or a **DFDS Seaways** ferry from Oslo in Norway. There are no direct ferry routes between the UK and Denmark.

Travelling by Public Transport

Arriva buses, DSB local trains and **Metro Service** rapid transit systems are fast and reliable, with certain routes running 24/7. You can take a bike for free onto S-trains (S-tog), but there are generally peak-hour restrictions on the Metro. In Greater Copenhagen, you can use a single ticket or buy a **Rejsekort**, a prepaid smart card that can be topped up and used on all three systems. Smart cards work out cheaper than individual tickets, but you can only purchase them from stations. Most S-tog stations have a 7/11 convenience store doubling as a ticket office. Be careful when entering and exiting the bus, as you may cross a bike lane and bikes have the right of way.

Travelling by Harbour Bus

Harbour buses (991, 992, 993) run the length of the city's harbour between Nordre Toldbod (near the Gefionspringvandet fountain), past Den Sorte Diamant to Teglholmen, south of Fisketorvet. They run from 7am to 7pm Monday to Friday, and from 10am Saturday to Sunday, roughly every 15 minutes at peak times and hourly at other times. Harbour buses use the same ticket or card as other modes of transport.

Travelling by Car

You can drive in Denmark if you are over 18 and hold a valid licence. Always carry the registration papers and a reflecting triangle – and always watch out for cyclists. There are several good car share schemes in operation around the city, the most popular being **Drive Now** and **LetsGo**, which offer a very good, cost-effective way of travelling long distances with larger groups. In Copenhagen, on-street parking in the city centre can be a challenge, and car parks are expensive. There are many parking apps, including **Easypark**, **Parkman** or **Parkpark**, which use your mobile phone's GPS to pinpoint your spot, and also enable you to pay online using a credit card; often this is easier than trying to find a ticket machine. The street sign "Parkering forbudt" means no parking within certain time limits. Note that motoring offences attract on-the-spot fines.

Travelling by Taxi and Rickshaw

Available taxis have a "fri" (free) sign on the roof, but hailing one can prove a challenge. It can often be quicker to find a taxi rank; most S-train and Metro stations have one nearby. The biggest firms in Denmark are **TaxiNord** and **DanTaxi**; both offer a credit card payment option and receipts. **Uber** is also widespread. For an open-air ride, you can catch the cycle rickshaws for relatively short rides from Storkespringvandet, Tivoli, Rådhuspladsen and Nyhavn, but beware – this method of transport can be rather expensive.

Travelling by Bus and Boat

Enjoy the city at your own pace with the **Stromma** (check website) hop-on-hop-off bus tour, which covers all the city's top tourist hotspots. You can also explore Copenhagen's charming canals by boat.

Tours depart from Nyhavn and Holmens Kanal, and you can choose either an hour-long grand tour or a hop-on-hop-off flexible day pass. Stromma, in Nyhavn, offers the biggest choice of tours, including some that have live music and on-board dining. **Netto Boats** (check website; tours in English, German, Danish), also in Nyhavn, is a slightly cheaper but an equally good alternative.

Travelling by Bicycle

Cycling is undoubtedly the best way to get around Copenhagen. The city boasts an unparalleled number of dedicated cycle paths. While it is not mandatory to wear a helmet while cycling, it is certainly recommended, especially in the city centre. It is illegal to cycle at night

without front and rear lights so make sure your rental bike is fitted with both; a bell can be handy, too. **Bycyklen** offers bicycles for rent at 30 Dkr per hour. These are available year-round from stands across the city, and have a built-in sat-nav system. You must register online before you can use them. Stick to the cycle paths if available, and always stop to allow passengers onto and off buses.

Travelling on Foot

Copenhagen is compact and flat, making it a joy to explore on foot. Many of the sights, especially those in the city centre, are just a short walk away from one other. Be sure that you do not confuse bike lanes with pedestrian pavements as this can be a painful mistake.

DIRECTORY

ARRIVING BY AIR

British Airways
📞 70 12 80 22
🌐 britishairways.com

Copenhagen Airport
🌐 cph.dk/en

easyJet
📞 89 88 10 32
🌐 easyjet.com

Norwegian
📞 70 80 78 80
🌐 norwegian.com

Scandinavian Airlines
📞 70 10 20 00 🌐 sas.dk

ARRIVING BY TRAIN

Danish State Railways
📞 70 13 14 15 🌐 dsb.dk

ARRIVING BY ROAD

Great Belt Bridge
🌐 storebaelt.dk

Øresund Bridge
🌐 oresundsbron.com

ARRIVING BY FERRY

DFDS Seaways
🌐 dfdsseaways.co.uk

Polferries
🌐 polferries.com

TRAVELLING BY PUBLIC TRANSPORT

Arriva
📞 72 30 25 00
🌐 arriva.dk

Metro Service
📞 70 15 16 15 🌐 m.dk

Rejsekort
🌐 rejsekort.dk

TRAVELLING BY CAR

DriveNow
🌐 drive-now.com

Easypark
🌐 easypark.dk

LetsGo
🌐 letsgo.dk

Parkman
🌐 parkman.dk

Parkpark
🌐 parkpark.dk

TRAVELLING BY TAXI

DanTaxi
📞 70 25 25 25
🌐 dantaxi.dk

TaxiNord
📞 48 48 48 48
🌐 taxinord.dk

Uber
🌐 uber.com/en-No/cities/copenhagen

TRAVELLING BY BUS AND BOAT

Netto Boats
📞 32 54 41 02
🌐 havnerundfart.dk

Stromma
📞 32 96 30 00
🌐 stromma.dk

TRAVELLING BY BICYCLE

Bycyklen
🌐 bycyklen.dk

Practical Information

Passports and Visas

Visitors from outside the European Economic Area (EEA), European Union (EU) and Switzerland need a valid passport to travel to Denmark, as do UK visitors. Swiss, EEA and EU nationals can use identity cards instead. Visitors from Canada, the US, Australia and New Zealand can stay for up to 90 days without a visa, as long as their passport is valid for 6 months beyond the date of entry. A visa is necessary for longer stays and must be obtained in advance from the Danish embassy (Schengen visas are valid). All other visitors need valid passports and visas. The **Ministry of Foreign Affairs** has up-to-date details. Most countries have consular representation in Copenhagen, including **Australia**, the **UK**, **Canada** and the **US**.

Customs and Immigration

Denmark imposes strict limits on what can be imported. Do not carry food items that have not been vacuum-packed by the manufacturer. Items in commercial quantities and gifts valued at more than 1,350 Dkr are also subject to customs duty. US citizens are liable to pay duty if carrying goods worth more than $400.

Travel Safety Advice

Visitors can get up-to-date travel safety information from the **UK Foreign and Commonwealth Office**, the **US Department of State** and the **Australian Department of Foreign Affairs and Trade**.

Travel Insurance

Do not travel without valid insurance, and be sure to check the policy's details, particularly how much you can claim for the loss of individual items. If you require medical treatment you may have to pay and claim it back later.

Health

Tourists are covered by public health services if there is an agreement between Denmark and their home country. EU nationals should carry a valid **EHIC** (European Health Insurance Card). Emergency treatment is free, unless the hospital concludes that the emergency was the result of a pre-existing condition. **Rigshospitalet** is a good hospital for urgent care, while **Bispebjerg Hospital** has an A&E department. If you require emergency dental treatment, head to **Dentist Tandlægevagten**. Doctors' fee refunds can be obtained at the nearest municipal or health insurance office. Prescription medication can be bought at pharmacies (apotek), denoted by a green "A" sign. Credit cards are not accepted. **Steno Apotek** is open 24/7.

Personal Security

Copenhagen is a safe city, but visitors must take precautions. Make sure your credit cards, mobile phone and cash are kept in a safe place, and be wary of pickpockets on public transport, particularly on crowded Metro trains. If you are a victim of a crime, contact the **Central Police Station** to file a report. You will be given a crime report note, which you will need for any insurance claims.

Emergency Services

In a crisis situation, or if you witness a serious crime, call **emergency** services immediately.

Travellers With Specific Needs

Copenhagen is a relatively accessible city, although some shops and restaurants in the older parts of the city centre do not offer facilities for those with specific needs. While the city is almost completely flat, its cobblestone roads can be a challenge for wheelchairs. All public transport, however, is accessible. **DSB Handicap Service** has useful information on public transport accessibility, and the **Visit Copenhagen** office lists places that offer facilities for the disabled.

Travelling With Children

Several museums have children's facilities and exhibitions for younger visitors. Most restaurants provide high chairs and children's menus, but not all offer baby-changing facilities. The two major department stores, **ILLUM** (see p73) and **Magasin du Nord** (see pp22–3), have play and baby-changing areas. The airport has buggies for use in the terminal, and baby-changing and play areas. Prams can be taken on public transport for free (buses only have space for two at a time).

Currency and Banking

Denmark is not part of the eurozone, and while some shops will accept euros, the local currency (Danish kroner) is usually preferred. Danish notes come in denominations of 1,000 Dkr, 500 Dkr, 200 Dkr, 100 Dkr and 50 Dkr, while coins are 20 Dkr, 10 Dkr, 5 Dkr, 2 Dkr, 1 Dkr and 50 øre (half a krone). Banks open 10am to 4pm Monday to Wednesday and 10am to 5pm or 5:30pm Thursday. Most ATMs are open 24/7, and are usually found outside banks and Metro stations. Using Visa, MasterCard or American Express cards is not a problem. Some smaller shops will only accept Dankort (a debit card only available to Danes), so it is best to always carry some cash. There are many exchange bureaux across the city; those open longest include the **Forex** (8am–9pm) at the central station and the **Danske Bank** exchange office (6am–10pm) at the airport. Many hotels exchange money, but the rate can be much lower than at official exchange bureaux.

Telephone and Internet

The international dialling code for Denmark is +45; there are no area codes. To make international calls from Denmark, first dial 00. Public telephones accept coins and phone-cards. Insert 5–20 Dkr for international calls, but note you will not receive change. GSM-compatible mobile phones will work, and 4G network coverage is excellent in most of the city. The main service providers are **TDC**, **Telenor** and **Telia**. Check your service provider's roaming rates before you travel though. Most hotels offer internet access and Wi-Fi. Many trains and buses and some public spaces have free Wi-Fi.

DIRECTORY

PASSPORTS AND VISAS

Australia
Dampfaergevej 26
w denmark.embassy.gov.au

Canada
Kristen Bernikowsgade 1
w denmark.gc.ca

Ministry of Foreign Affairs
w um.dk/en

UK
Kastelsvej 36–40
w ukindenmark.fco.gov.uk

US
Dag Hammarskjölds Allé 24
w dk.usembassy.gov

TRAVEL SAFETY ADVICE

Australian Department of Foreign Affairs and Trade
w dfat.gov.au
w smartraveller.gov.au

UK Foreign and Commonwealth Office
w gov.uk/foreign-travel-advice

US Department of State
w travel.state.gov

HEALTH

Bispebjerg Hospital
w bispebjerghospital.dk

Dentist
Tandlægevagten
w dentalklinikken.dk

EHIC
w nhs.uk/ehic

Rigshospitalet
w rigshospitalet.dk

Steno Apotek
w stenoapotek.dk

PERSONAL SECURITY

Central Police Station
C 33 14 14 48

EMERGENCY SERVICES

Emergency
C 112/114

TRAVELLERS WITH SPECIFIC NEEDS

DSB Handicap Service
C 70 13 14 15

Visit Copenhagen
Vesterbrogade 4
w visitcopenhagen.com

CURRENCY AND BANKING

Danske Bank
w danskebank.com

Forex
w forexbank.dk/en

TELEPHONE AND INTERNET

TDC
C 70 70 30 30
w tdc.dk

Telenor
C 72 10 01 00
w telenor.dk

Telia
C 80 40 44 44
w telia.dk

Postal Services

Post offices are open 9 or 10am to 5:30pm Monday to Friday (timings vary between post offices) and 9am to noon Saturday. In the city centre, **Posthus Pilestræde** is a convenient post office; **Posthus Østerbro** is in Østerbro. International mail arrives faster with the Prioritaire mail or Faste Deliver A-mail service, but this can be expensive. Check the **PostNord** website for current rates.

Television, Radio and Newspapers

Cable and satellite TV offer channels in English and other languages, and most of the US and UK programmes broadcast by Danish networks are in English with Danish subtitles. **DR Radio** does not broadcast current affairs in English, but it does update its website with the news in English. Denmark's national newspapers include *Politiken*, *Børsen*, and *Information*; for local news in English, pick up a copy of the *Copenhagen Post* (published Friday). You can find most major UK and US newspapers at the airport, central station and in some city centre kiosks. English news website thelocal.dk is useful for current events.

Opening Hours

Shops are open 9:30 or 10am to 5:30pm Monday to Thursday, 9:30 or 10am to 7 or 8pm Friday and 9:30 or 10am to 3pm Saturday (to 5pm on the first Saturday of the month). Since the trading laws have been relaxed, larger shops now open on Sundays. You may find weekend hours extended in tourist areas, especially during summer.

Time Difference

Copenhagen is on Central European Time (CET), which is an hour ahead of London, six hours ahead of New York, nine hours ahead of Los Angeles and eight hours behind Sydney.

Electrical Appliances

You can use your electric appliances in Denmark if the standard voltage in your country is in the range of 220–240 volts. If it is in the range of 100–127 volts (as in the US, Canada and most South American countries), you will need a voltage converter. Sockets take standard European double round-pin plugs, so you may also need to use a plug adaptor.

Driving

To hire a car you need to be over 20 years old and have held a full driving licence for at least a year. To pick up the car, you will need your passport and a credit card to pay the security deposit. You may also need an International Driving Permit (IDP).

Weather

Denmark has a rather temperate climate, with no extremes of heat or cold, but the weather can be very changeable. July and August are the two hottest and sunniest months in Copenhagen, with temperatures of 19° C (68° F), while the months of January and February are the coldest, with temperatures of 2° C (35° F). The best times to visit are the summer, when you can enjoy as many as 16–18 hours of daylight on clear days, and Christmas, which is when the concept of hygge really comes into its own. The only time you might want to avoid visiting – due to chilly winds and limited daylight hours (just 7) – is January.

Visitor Information

The **Visit Copenhagen** *(see p111)* tourist office is close to the central railway station and offers a wealth of visitor information, as well as hotel bookings, car hire, the **Copenhagen Card** and information about tours. The *Copenhagen Post* lists all the arts, music and cultural events taking place across the city, while Danish-speakers can check the Friday guide sections of daily newspapers *Politiken* and *Berlingske*. The **Visit Denmark**, **Copenhagen Tourist** and **Visit Copenhagen** websites have plenty of information.

Shopping

What it lacks in size, the main shopping district makes up for in quality and variety. Few capitals can match the dizzying array of independent stores and high-end boutiques on offer, and the city centre also boasts two major department stores: **Magasin du Nord** (see pp22–3) and **ILLUM** (see p73). The biggest stores are located on **Strøget** (see p62), Europe's longest pedestrianized street. Shoppers should head to **Royal Copenhagen** (see p73) for exclusive porcelain, **Birger Christensen** (see p73) for high-end designer fashion and **Illums Bolighus** (see p73) for beautiful Danish-designed homewares.

Venturing off the beaten track is just as rewarding; **Kronprinsensgade** (see p62) in the city centre is great for Danish fashion and streetwear, while unique **Ravnsborggade** in Nørrebro is the perfect place for antique-hunting.

If malls are more your thing, hop on the Metro to **Field's** in Ørestaden, or take a ride on the S-tog to Dybbølsbro Station for **Fisketorvet Copenhagen Mall** (see p62). Prices can often be eye-wateringly expensive, but there are frequent sales. Look out for signs saying *slutspurt*, *lagersalg* or *udsalg* to find good bargains.

Dining

You're spoilt for choice in terms of dining options in Copenhagen. The city is home to some of the best restaurants in the world, and while you may not find the same variety of international cuisine you would in, for example, London, it is difficult to find a poor-quality eatery.

Most restaurants will open for dinner at around 6pm, with kitchens typically closing at around 10 or 10:30pm. Booking is always strongly advised, especially if you're planning on dining out on

Friday and Saturday evenings, as eating out is one of the Danes' favourite things to do.

Most restaurants in the city are child-friendly, but families with babies and toddlers are advised to check ahead that high chairs and baby-changing facilities are available.

Menu prices are high, and it can often be difficult to find a reasonably priced bottle of wine, even in lower-priced restaurants. Look out for early bird deals, and if you're travelling in the month of October, take advantage of **Copenhagen Dining Week**, during which hundreds of restaurants across the city offer popular cut-price menus.

Accommodation

Copenhagen has a wide range of accommodation available, but be aware that it does not come cheap. Make sure you do your research and book well in advance. Weekend stays in hotels can be cheaper than weekdays. If money is not an issue, you'll find plenty of high-end hotels scattered across the city, the most exclusive being the popular five-star **Hotel d'Angleterre** (see p114), which enjoys a prime location on Kongens Nytorv and boasts its own in-house spa.

A more affordable and often authentic option is to rent an apartment via **Airbnb** – you'll find thousands across the city. **Couchsurfing** is another popular way of meeting locals and staying in the city without spending a huge amount of money.

DIRECTORY

POSTAL SERVICES

Posthus Østerbro
Øster Allé 1
[70 70 70 30

Posthus Pilestræde
Pilestræde 58
[70 70 70 30

PostNord
w postnord.com

TELEVISION, RADIO AND NEWSPAPERS

Børsen
w børsen.dk

Copenhagen Post
w cphpost.dk

DR Radio
w dr.dk/radio

Information
w information.dk

Politiken
w politiken.dk

VISITOR INFORMATION

Berlingske
w b.dk

Copenhagen Card
w copenhagencard.com

Copenhagen Tourist
w cph-tourist.dk

Visit Copenhagen
w visitcopenhagen.com

Visit Denmark
w denmark.dk

SHOPPING

Field's
w fields.dk

Ravnsborggade
w ravnsborggade.dk

DINING

Copenhagen Dining Week
w diningweek.dk

ACCOMMODATION

Airbnb
w airbnb.com

Couchsurfing
w couchsurfing.com

Places to Stay

PRICE CATEGORIES
For a standard double room per night (with breakfast if included), taxes and extra charges.

(Kr) under 1,000 (Kr)(Kr) 1,000–1,600 (Kr)(Kr)(Kr) over 1,600

Luxury Hotels

Hotel Front

MAP L4 ▪ Skt Annæ Plads 21 ▪ 33 13 34 00 ▪ www. scandichotels.dk/front ▪ (Kr)(Kr)

Child-friendly hotels can be hard to come by, but this place offers rooms of various sizes. Each room has been uniquely decorated to embrace a cozy and residential feeling.

Skt. Petri

MAP H4 ▪ Krystalgade 22 ▪ 33 45 91 00 ▪ www. sktpetri.com ▪ (Kr)(Kr)(Kr)

Housed in a landmark heritage building in a fantastic location in the historic Latin Quarter, this modern hotel has two restaurants and a wine bar. There's also a garden courtyard and a fitness studio.

Copenhagen Plaza

MAP G5 ▪ Bernstorffsgade 4 ▪ 33 14 92 62 ▪ www. ligula.se/profilhotels/ copenhagen-plaza ▪ (Kr)(Kr)(Kr)(Kr)

Built in 1913, this historic hotel has spacious rooms and traditional decor. The Library Bar, packed with 18th-century books, is one of the city's best spots for a nightcap.

Hotel d'Angleterre

MAP K4 ▪ Kongens Nytorv 34 ▪ 33 12 00 95 ▪ www. dangleterre.dk ▪ (Kr)(Kr)(Kr)(Kr)

Olden-day grandeur meets modern luxury at this hotel. It has a plush palm court, banquet rooms, a spa and an elegant restaurant.

Manon Les Suites

MAP G4 ▪ Gyldenløvesgade 19 ▪ 45 70 00 15 ▪ www. guldsmedenhotels.com/ manon-les-suites ▪ (Kr)(Kr)(Kr)

Manon offers 82 suites, each ideal for a family or five people. The hotel emphasizes sustainability, from daily operations to organic food and beauty products. Room decor is distinctly hip with a mid-century modern flavour.

Nimb Hotel

MAP G5 ▪ Bernstorffsgade 5 ▪ 88 70 00 00 ▪ www. nimb.dk ▪ (Kr)(Kr)(Kr)

One of the most exclusive hotels in Copenhagen, Nimb has 38 rooms. Each of the rooms is unique and luxurious, and features range from open fireplaces to flatscreen TVs. Housed in the landmark Nimb building, and with its own private limousine service, this is A-list accommodation.

Nyhavn 71

MAP L4 ▪ Nyhavn 71 ▪ 33 43 62 00 ▪ www. 71nyhavnhotel.com ▪ (Kr)(Kr)(Kr)(Kr)

This charming four-star hotel was once a warehouse built to store goods from ships in the harbour. The area is very peaceful even though it is located near the most popular canal in Copenhagen.

Palace Hotel

MAP H5 ▪ Rådhuspladsen 57 ▪ 33 14 40 50 ▪ www. scandichotels.com/ hotels/denmark/ copenhagen/scandic-palace ▪ (Kr)(Kr)(Kr)

Rooms at this Victorian hotel are decorated in an English style but have a modern twist. Celebrities like Judy Garland, Audrey Hepburn and Errol Flynn have added a touch of glamour to the hotel.

Boutique Hotels

Avenue Hotel

MAP C4 ▪ Åboulevard 29 ▪ 35 37 31 11 ▪ www. brochner-hotels.dk/hotel-avenue-copenhagen ▪ (Kr)(Kr)

This boutique hotel is located on the edge of Frederiksberg, close to both the Lakes and the lively Nørrebro district. A hotel since 1939, it offers child-friendly, spacious family rooms. Breakfast can be enjoyed on the terrace, which also has a child's sandpit.

Hotel SP34

MAP G4 ▪ Sankt Peders Stræde 34 ▪ 33 13 30 00 ▪ www.brochner-hotels. dk ▪ (Kr)(Kr)

This stylish boutique hotel is located in the Latin Quarter, not far from Rådhuspladsen. There are 118 beautifully furnished rooms, all with free Wi-Fi and cable TV. The hotel has two good restaurants, a lounge bar, a café and a terrace.

Axel Guldsmeden
MAP G6 ▪
Helgolandsgade 11
▪ 33 31 32 66 ▪ www.
hotelguldsmeden.dk
▪ ⓀⓀⓀ
This boutique eco-hotel is a surprising find close to the main train station. Relax in the saunas and steam baths of the hotel spa and enjoy excellent organic breakfasts in the heated courtyard.

Babette Guldsmeden
MAP L2 ▪ Bredgade 78
▪ 33 48 10 00 ▪ www.
guldsmedenhotels.com
▪ ⓀⓀⓀ
In a very peaceful location close to the green area of Kastellet [see p80], this green-certified hotel is inside a 19th-century building. Services include free organic coffee and a full service restaurant.

Carlton 66 Guldsmeden
MAP C5 ▪ Vesterbrogade 66 ▪ 33 22 15 00 ▪ www.
hotelguldsmeden.dk
▪ Ⓘ ⓀⓀⓀ
Sophisticated yet relaxed, this hotel has ethnic decor with dark-wood furniture, whitewashed walls and Egyptian cotton sheets. Breakfasts are delicious and organic.

Hotel Alexandra
MAP G5 ▪ H C Andersens Boulevard 8 ▪ 33 74 44 44 ▪ www.hotelalexandra.dk
▪ ⓀⓀⓀ
This excellent hotel has been around for more than a century and is popular for its original, furniture from the 50s–70s, with design classics ranging from Kaare Klint chairs to bespoke Akademi chandeliers designed by artist Poul Henningsen.

All second floor rooms are non-smoking and are safe for those with allergies.

Hotel Sanders
MAP K4
▪ Tordenskjoldsgade 15
▪ 46 40 00 40 ▪ www.
hotelsanders.com
▪ ⓀⓀⓀ
This five-storey luxury boutique hotel is housed in a Jugendstil building from the 1860s. Rooms range from snug to very spacious. The magnificent interior features bespoke Colonial furniture and Danish classic design.

Hotel Twentyseven
MAP H5 ▪ Løngangstræde 27 ▪ 70 27 56 27 ▪ www.
firsthotels.com ▪ ⓀⓀⓀ
This boutique hotel, with its minimalist decor, is centrally located not far from Rådhuspladsen and Strøget. The hotel bars include a wine bar, a cocktail lounge and the Icebar Copenhagen.

Imperial Hotel
MAP G5 ▪ Vester Farimagsgade 9 ▪ 33 12 80 00 ▪ www.imperial-hotel-copenhagen.com
▪ ⓀⓀⓀ
Stylish and welcoming, this four-star hotel has been decorated in modern Danish design and has an entire floor dedicated to the work of late Danish designer Børge Mogensen.

Mid-Range Hotels

Savoy
MAP C5 ▪ Vesterbrogade 34 ▪ 33 26 75 00 ▪ www.
savoyhotel.dk ▪ Ⓚ
Dating from 1906, this 66-room hotel is known for its distinctive Art Nouveau façade, and is a Vesterbro landmark.

Renovated but still affordably priced, it has Wi-Fi in all rooms and a guest PC in the lobby. The rooms facing the courtyard are much quieter.

Ibsens Hotel
MAP G3 ▪ Vendersgade 23 ▪ 33 13 19 13 ▪ www.
arthurhotels.dk/ibsens-hotel ▪ ⓀⓀ
This hotel is located in the Nansensgade area, a short walk away from Nørreport station and the food market. All rooms are decorated in modern Scandinavian style.

First Hotel Mayfair
MAP G6
▪ Helgolandsgade 3
▪ 70 12 17 00 ▪ www.
firsthotels.com ▪ ⓀⓀⓀ
Close to the city's main attractions, this hotel is furnished mainly in an English style with a hint of the Oriental.

The Square
MAP H5 ▪ Rådhuspladsen 14 ▪ 33 38 12 00 ▪ www.
thesquarecopenhagen.com ▪ ⓀⓀⓀ
This three-star hotel is located on the Town Hall square. It comes with stylish pony-hair chairs at the entrance and Arne Jacobsen chairs in the reception area. The breakfast is excellent.

Tivoli Hotel
MAP D6 ▪ Arni Magnussons Gade 2
▪ 44 87 00 00 ▪ www.
tivolihotel.com ▪ ⓀⓀⓀ
This high-rise hotel has activities for kids, as well as a pool and fitness centre. Part of the Tivoli Congress Center, it also caters for business guests. A free shuttle bus operates between the hotel and Tivoli.

Rooms with a View

Danhostel Copenhagen City
MAP J6 ■ H C Andersens Blvd 50 ■ 33 11 85 85 ■ www.danhostel.dk/ copenhagencity ■ Ⓚ
This modern and design-led Danhostel is one of the biggest in the city. It is located close to Tivoli and Rådhuspladsen.

Copenhagen Island
MAP J6 ■ Kalvebod Brygge 53 ■ 33 38 96 00 ■ www.copenhagenisland. com ■ ⓀⓀ
This beautiful state-of-the-art hotel is on an island in the middle of Copenhagen harbour. Architect Kim Utzon's extraordinary building places a great emphasis on the play of glass and light. The rooms offer scenic views of the Sound. It also has its own, very well-equipped gym and fitness centre.

Dragør Badehotel
MAP C3 ■ Drogdensvej 43, Dragør ■ 32 53 05 00 ■ www.badehotellet.dk ■ ⓀⓀ
The fishing village of Dragør is popular with tourists and this hotel's rooms have good views of the sea and countryside.

Kurhotel Skodsborg
MAP B2 ■ Skodsborg Strandvej 139, Skodsborg ■ 45 58 58 00 ■ www.skodsborg.dk ■ ⓀⓀ
Once a summer palace, this century-old health resort is a beautiful place to stay. Overlooking the sea, it is perfect for health and fitness fanatics, with a good range of therapies and fitness programmes, plus healthy food.

Skovshoved Hotel
MAP B2 ■ Strandvejen 267, Charlottenlund ■ 39 64 00 28 ■ www.skovshovedhotel.com ■ ⓀⓀ
Away from the bustle of central Copenhagen, this elegant seaside hotel is more than 350 years old. Tastefully decorated in a Scandinavian style, it is surrounded by fisher-men's houses and offers beautiful views. The restaurant is mentioned in the Michelin Guide, so be sure to book ahead.

Admiral
MAP L3 ■ Toldbodgade 24–8 ■ 33 74 14 14 ■ www.admiralhotel.dk ■ ⓀⓀⓀ
Originally an 18th-century granary, this splendid four-star hotel in the city centre is within easy reach of shopping areas, theatres and other attractions. Its rooms offer stunning views of the Operaen (see pp94–5). The foyer has models of ships. The restaurant, Salt, is excellent.

Copenhagen Strand
MAP L4 ■ Havnegade 37 ■ 33 48 99 00 ■ www.copenhagenstrand.com ■ ⓀⓀⓀ
This three-star hotel is housed in a lovely 1869 harbourfront warehouse, tucked away on a pretty, quiet street opposite the Christianshavns canal. The decor is rustic and the view is wonderful.

Hotel CPHLIVING
MAP J6 ■ Langebrogade 1A ■ 61 60 85 46 ■ www.cphliving.com ■ ⓀⓀⓀ
Copenhagen's first floating hotel is built on a barge and located in the center of the inner harbour in the center of the city. There are 12 rooms, all with views of the old town and harbour.

Radisson Blu Royal Hotel
MAP G5 ■ Hammerichsgade 1 ■ 33 42 60 00 ■ www.radisson.com ■ ⓀⓀⓀ
This famous Radisson hotel, designed by Arne Jacobsen in the 1950s, is packed with five-star comforts. The rooms afford great views over the city. Café Royal on the 20th floor serves high-end cuisine and afternooon tea.

Budget Hotels

CabInn City
MAP H6 ■ Mitchellsgade 14 ■ 33 46 16 16 ■ www.cabinn.com ■ Ⓚ
Based on the idea of a ship's cabin, the rooms at CabInn City are small but perfectly designed, with all the modern conveni-ences tucked into a clever storage design. You can pick from bunk beds in twin rooms, double rooms and family rooms. The hotel has a pleasant ambience and every morning there is a very good buffet breakfast.

CabInn Metro
MAP H6 ■ Arne Jakobsens Allé 2 ■ 32 46 57 00 ■ www.cabinn.com ■ Ⓚ
The Metro is the fourth hotel in the city's budget Cab Inn concept, and is Denmark's largest hotel. It is located very close to the city's airport and Field's shopping centre. All 710 rooms are modern and clean, and all have en-suite facilities. Free Wi-Fi access is always included in the room rate.

CabInn Scandinavia

MAP C4 ■ Vodroffsvej 55, Frederiksberg ■ 35 36 11 11 ■ www.cabinn.com ■ ⓚ

This CabInn hotel is located just a block away from the CabInn Express and a road before the Peblinge Lake. It is equipped with all the modern conveniences found at the other three CabInns in the city.

Generator Hostel Copenhagen

MAP K3 ■ Adelgade 5–7 ■ 78 77 54 00 ■ www. generatorhostels.com ■ ⓚ

A smart, modern hostel with private, en-suite rooms as well as dorms. Facilities include Wi-Fi, a bar and breakfast (for an extra charge).

Hotel Copenhagen

MAP E6 ■ Egilsgade 33, Islands Brygge ■ 32 96 27 27 ■ www.hotel copenhagen.dk ■ ⓚ

Just a few minutes away from the city centre by Metro, this hotel offers rooms sleeping up to four with shared bathrooms. There are also some very nice rooms with en-suite facilities. Free Wi-Fi is available in the reception and, for a small charge, a breakfast can be ordered when you book.

Wakeup Copenhagen Borgergade

MAP K3 ■ Borgergade 9 ■ 44 80 00 90 ■ www. wakeupcopenhagen.dk ■ ⓚ

This 498-room hotel offers ultramodern accommodation just minutes from Kongens Nytorv, Amalienborg and other city-centre sights. The interior is extremely stylish and part of a new generation of budget accommodation appearing in the city.

Wakeup Copenhagen Carsten Niebuhrs Gade

MAP D6 ■ Carsten Niebuhrs Gade 11 ■ 44 80 00 10 ■ www.wakeup copenhagen.dk ■ ⓚ

Designed by Kim Utzon, this ultramodern, two-star budget hotel is located along the waterfront, close to Fisketorvet shopping mall. Its 510 rooms are spread over 12 floors, with prices rising per floor.

Other Accommodation

Copenhagen Downtown Hostel

MAP J5 ■ Vandkunsten 5 ■ 70 23 21 10 ■ www. copenhagendowntown. com ■ ⓚ

Located right in the heart of the city, this hostel promises a vibrant and artistic international atmosphere. It has a café, lounge and restaurant. In addition to the dorm and four-bedded rooms, there are rooms for two to three people with en-suite facilities. A YHA membership card is required, but this can be purchased when checking in.

DCU-Copenhagen Camp "Absalon" UK

Korsdalsvej 132, DK-2610 Rødovre ■ 36 41 06 00 ■ www.dcu.dk ■ ⓚ

Visitors can park their caravans here or sleep in tents. There are also 45 cabins, most with en-suite facilities. There are recreational areas including a playground with bouncing cushions and chess here. Guests also get access to Wi-Fi.

Steel House Copenhagen

MAP C5 ■ Herholdtsgade 6 ■ 33 17 71 10 ■ www. steelhousecopenhagen. com ■ ⓚ

This 253-room hostel, opened in summer 2017, is a stone's throw from the Vesterport Station. Sleek rooms range from 6- and 4-bed dorms to single rooms. In addition to a self-service kitchen and cool craft-beer bar, there are sports facilities, a café, reading lounge, business centre, pool and music venue.

Apartment in Copenhagen

MAP E4 ■ Hindegade 6 ■ 77 34 56 45 ■ www. apartmentincopenhagen. com ■ ⓚⓚⓚ

Agency specializing in short- and long-term lets in smart, furnished apartments at attractive city locations, for couples and for families.

STAY Apartment Hotel

MAP D6 ■ Islands Brygge 79A ■ 72 44 44 34 ■ www.staycopenhagen. dk ■ ⓚⓚⓚ

A stunning-looking building renovated by the designers of Hay House (see p73), STAY offers serviced apartments with superb waterfront views. The building also houses an excellent small Italian restaurant, an organic supermarket and a very good gourmet bakery.

General Index

Acknowledgments

Author
Antonia Cunningham

Additional contributor
Chris Moss

Publishing Director Georgina Dee

Publisher Vivien Antwi

Design Director Phil Ormerod

Editorial Ankita Awasthi Tröger, Rachel Fox, Maresa Manara, Alison McGill, Lucy Richards, Sally Schafer, Hollie Teague

Cover Design Maxine Pedliham, Vinita Venugopal

Design Tessa Bindloss, Bharti Karakoti

Picture Research Susie Peachey, Ellen Root, Lucy Sienkowska

Cartography Subhashree Bharati, Suresh Kumar, Casper Morris

DTP Jason Little

Production Luca Bazzoli

Factchecker Taraneh Jerven

Proofreader Kathryn Glendenning

Indexer Hilary Bird

Revisions Avanika, Sumita Khatwani, Shikha Kulkarni, Gaurav Nagpal, Kathleen Sauret, Azeem Siddiqui, Beverly Smart, Vaishali Vashisht

Picture Credits

108: Freya Mcomish 97cra.

123RF.com: bloodua 12bl; Oliver Förstner 87br; Chon Kit Leong 78bc; scanrail 23tl, 68tl; Figurniy Sergey 80cla.

Alamy Stock Photo: Arco Images / Di Rosa, G. 22bl; Jon Bilous 4cla; Richard Cummins 30–1c; Directphoto Collection 32cra; Entertainment Pictures 47tr; Greg Balfour Evans 4clb; Oliver Förstner 98cla; Hemis 17cr; Hemis / Bertrand Gardel 30bl; Nigel Howard 90t; imageBROKER / NielsDK 19tl; John Peter Photography 93bl; Heini Kettunen 78t; Paul Maguire 4cl; Martin Norris Travel Photography 3tr, 106–107; Kim Petersen 42bl; Niels Poulsen mou 70tr; Niels Quist 28br, 96br; Realimage 20–21; Jani Riekkinen 4crb; Jonathan Smith 31crb; The Picture Art Collection 37cl; VWPics 57cl.

Aurum: 96ca.

Bakkehuset: 46br, 89cl.

Bakken Kbh: Polina Vinogradova 56br.

Brus Bar: 82cla

Copenhagen Media Center: Klaus Bentzen 64–5; Wallmans Cirkusbygningen 54; Copenhagen Jazz Festival / Jonas Pryner 55tr; Den Røde Cottage 105cr; Rasmus Flindt Pedersen 75br; Restaurant Kong Hans Kælder 61cl; Johan Rosenmunthe 88tr; Ty Stange 64tl, 65cla; Strömma Danmark 72br; Ulf Svane / The Spoon Company 65tr; Torvehallerne Kbh 63cl.

Copenhagen Pride Festival: Anders Jung 59tr.

Danish Royal Palaces: Thomas Rahbek 101cl, 104b.

Den Blå Planet: Bjarke MacCarthy 53cra, 100tl.

Designmuseum Danmark: Pernille Klemp 76tl.

DR Koncerthuset: David Borland Architectural Photography 55cl.

Dreamstime.com: Albo 11b; Anderm 41cl; Andrey Andronov 38t; Leonid Andronov 16bl, 18–19, 70–71; Aurinko 24cl, 39cra, 80br; Jon Bilous 29tl; Bloodua 10tl; Collette Branco 69tl; Deanpictures 75c; Dennis Dolkens 77br; Michal Durinik 41tr; Igor Dymov 94bl; Eugenephoen 6tr, 42t; Oliver Förstner 10clb, 19crb, 51crb; Gary718 7br; Giuseppemasci 102br; Dennis Jacobsen 38bl; Irina Lepneva 12–13; Mapics 6cla; Marinv 62b; Sophie Mcaulay 77tr; Jaroslav Moravcik 48–9; Ohmaymay 4b; Pavel Parmenov 50b; Pod666 25tl; Rndmst 72tc; Natalia Rumyantseva 18br, Igor Stojakovic 13crb, Parinya Suwanitch 22–3, Jason Vosper 46tl; Vvoevale 10bl; Zastavkin 11cr, 28cl, 40tl.

Fisketorv Shopping Centre: 62tr.

Formel B: 60bc.

Getty Images: BirgerNiss 37tr; Bloomberg 43cl; Cultura RM Exclusive / Atli Mar Hafsteinsson 87tl; DEA / A. Dagli Orti 36b, / G. Roli 36ca; Tim Graham 58–9; Annapurna Mellor 48tl; MyLoupe 45tr, /Universal Images Group 4cra.

iStockphoto.com: fotoVoyager 4t; krugli 93b; MissPassionPhotography 1; scanrail 2tl, 8–9; SeanPavonePhoto 3tl, 66–7.

The Jane: 56t.

Jazzhus Monmartre: Lars Gundersen 74t.

Georg Jensen AS, Denmark: Peter Krasilnikoff 63tr.

Kiin Kiin: 60t.

Kulturcentret Assistens: 47cl.

The Laundromat Cafe: 61tr.

Les Trois Cochons: Chris Tonnesen 91br.

Loppen: 29crb.

Louisiana Museum of Modern Art : Kim Hansen 103t.

Masken Bar & Café: 58tr.

Mikkeller: Theis Mortensen 50tl.

The Museum of National History at Frederiksborg Castle: 40–41, 100b; Mikkel Grønlund 84–5.

Nationalmuseet, Danmark: Roberto Fortuna and Kira Ursem 11clb, 33br; Lennart Larsen 32br; John Lee 33tr.

Normann Copenhagen: Jeppe Sørensen 81tr.

North Atlantic House: 94tr.

Ny Carlsberg Glyptotek: Ana Cecilia Gonzalez 2tr, 34–5, 44b.

Orangeriet Kongens Have: 83cla.

Ordrupgaard: Anders Sune Berg 99br.

Ripley Entertainment Inc: Copenhagen Guinness World Records Museum / Johanne Lerbech 52bl.

Royal Copenhagen Porcelain: Gab Admin 73cb.

The Royal Danish Theatre: Christophe Pelç 54b; Costin Radu 23crb; Egon Street 95cl.

Rust: 82b.

SMK – National Gallery of Denmark: 11cra, 26cla, 26br, 27tr, 45cl, 79cl.

Sticks 'n' Sushi: 91ca.

SuperStock: Yadid Levy 73cra.

Team Bade / Islands Brygge Harbour Bath: 13tl, 49tr.

The Danish Jewish Museum: 31tl; Josefine Amalie 44tl.

The Royal Danish Collection: 24cra; Iben Bolling Kaufmann 10crb, 16crb, 43br; Peter Norby 16–17, 17tl; Peter Nørby 11tl, 25crb, 25br.

Tivoli: Anders Bøggild 10c, 52t; Rasmus B. Hansen 15tl; Lasse Salling 14cla, 14bl, 14–15, 15br; Tivoli Gardens / Lasse Salling 69crb.

The Viking Ship Museum, Denmark: Werner Karrasch 99t, 102cla.

WarPigs Brewpub: Camilla Stephan & Rasmus Malmstr 57tr.

Zoologisk Have: Frank Ronsholt 49cl, 86cla; Frank Rønsholt 88b.

Cover

Front and spine: **iStockphoto.com:** MissPassionPhotography

Back: **Dreamstime.com:** Belier tl, Scanrail cla; **Getty Images:** Alexander Spatari; **iStockphoto.com:** MissPassionPhotography bc, pidjoe crb

Pull Out Map Cover

iStockphoto.com: MissPassionPhotography

All other images © Dorling Kindersley
For further information see:
www.dkimages.com

As a guide to abbreviations in visitor information blocks: ***Adm*** *= admission charge;* ***D*** *= dinner;* ***L*** *= lunch.*

MIX
Paper from
responsible sources
FSC
www.fsc.org   FSC™ C018179

Penguin
Random
House

Printed and bound in China

First edition 2007

Published in Great Britain
by Dorling Kindersley Limited
80 Strand, London WC2R 0RL

Published in the United States by
DK US, 1450 Broadway Suite 801,
New York, NY 10018, USA

Copyright © 2007, 2019 Dorling
Kindersley Limited

A Penguin Random House Company

19 20 21 22 10 9 8 7 6 5 4 3 2 1

**Reprinted with revisions 2009, 2011,
2013, 2015, 2018, 2019**

A CIP catalogue record is available
from the British Library.

A catalogue record for this book is available
from the Library of Congress.

ISSN 1479-344X

ISBN 978-0-2413-6493-2

Phrase Book

In an Emergency

Help!	Hjælp!	yellb!
Stop!	Stands!	stanns!
Can you call a doctor?	Kan du ringe til en læge?	kann do ringe-til ehn laiyeh?
Can you call an ambulance?	Kan du ringe til en ambulance?	kann do ringe-til ehn ahm-boo-lang-seh?
Can you call the police?	Kan du ringe til politiet?	kann do ringe-til po-ly-tee'd?
Can you call the fire brigade?	Kan du ringe til brand-væsenet?	kann do ringe-til brahn-vaiys-ned?
Is there a telephone here?	Er der en telefon i nærheden?	e-ah dah ehn tele-fohn ee neya-hethen?
Where is the nearest hospital?	Hvor er det nærmeste hospital?	voa e-ah deh neh-meste hoh-spee-tahl

Useful Phrases

Sorry	Undskyld	ons-gull
Goodnight	Godnat	goh-nad
Goodbye	Farvel	fah-vel
Good evening	Godaften	goh-ahf-tehn
Good morning	Godmorgen	goh-moh'n
Good day (after about 9am)	Goddag	goh-dah
Yes	Ja	yah
No	Nej	nye
Please	Værsgo/ Velbekomme	vehs-goh/ vell-beh-commeh
Thank you	Tak	tahgg
How are you?	Hvordan har du det?/ Hvordan går det?	voh-dann hah do deh?/ voh-dan go deh?
Well, thank you	Godt, tak	gohd, tahgg
Pleased to have met you	Det var rart at møde dig	deh vah rahd add meutheh die
See you!	Vi ses!	vee sehs!
I understand	Jeg forstår	yay fuh-stoah
I don't understand	Jeg forstår ikke	yay fuh-stoah egge
Does anyone speak English?	Er der nogen, der kan tale engelsk?	e-ah dah noh-enn dah kann tah-leh eng-ellsgg?
good	god	guth
bad	dårlig	doh-lee
up	op	ohb
down	ned	neth
near	tæt på	taid poh
far	langt fra	lahngd fra
on the left	til venstre	till vehn-streh
on the right	til højre	till hoy-reh
open	åben	oh-ben
closed	lukket	luh-geth
warm	varm	vahm
cold	kold	koll
big	stor	stoah
little	lille	lee-leh

Making a Telephone Call

English	Danish	Pronunciation
Whom am I speaking to?	Hvem taler jeg med?	vemm talah yay meth?
I would like to call...	Jeg vil gerne ringe til...	yay vill geh-neh ring-eh till...
I will telephone again	Jeg ringer en gang til	yay ring-ah ehn gahng till

In a Hotel

Do you have double rooms?	Findes her dobbelt-værelser?	feh-ness he-ah dob-belld vah-hel-sah?
With bathroom	Med bade-værelse	meth bah-the-vah-hel-sah
With washbasin	Med hånd-vask	meth hohn-vasgg
key	nøgle	noy-leh
I have a reservation	Jeg har en reservation	yay hah ehn res-sah-vah-shohn

Sightseeing

English	Danish	Pronunciation
entrance	indgang	ehn-gahng
exit	udgang	ooth-gahng
exhibition	udstilling	ooth-stelling
tourist information	turisto-plysning	tooh-reesd-ohb-lehs-ning
town/city hall	rådhus	rahd-hus
post office	posthus	posd-hus
cathedral	domkirke	dom-kia-keh
church	kirke	kia-keh
museum	museum	muh-seh-uhm
town bus	bybus	bih-boos
long-distance bus	rutebil	bus roo-teh-beel
railway station	banegård	bah-neh-goh
airport	lufthavn	luhft-havn
train	tog	toh
ferry terminal	færgehavn	fah-veh-havn
bus stop	busstoppested	buhs-sdob-beh-steth
long-distance bus station	rutebilstation	roo-teh-beel-sta-shion
a public toilet	et offentligt toilet	ehd off-end-ligd toa-led

Shopping

English	Danish	Pronunciation
I wish to buy...	Jeg vil gerne købe...	yay vill geh-neh kyh-beh...
Do you have...?	Findes der...?	feh-ness de-ah...?
How much does it cost?	Hvad koster det?	vath koh-stah deh
expensive	dyr	dyh-ah
cheap	billig	billy
size	størrelse	stoh-ell-seh
general store	købmand	keuhb-mann
greengrocer	grønthandler	grund-handla
supermarket	supermarked	suh-pah-mah-keth
market	marked	mah-keth

Eating Out

Do you have a table for... people?	Har I et bord til... personer?	hah ee ed boah till... peh-soh-nah?
I would like to sit by the window	Jeg vil gerne sidde ved vinduet	yay vill geh-neh saithe veth veen-do-ed

I wish to order...	**Jeg vil gerne bestille...**	*yay vill geh-neh beh-stilleh...*
I'm a vegetarian	**Jeg er vegetar**	*yay eh-ah veh-gehta*
children's menu	**børnemenu**	*byeh-neh-meh-nye*
daily special	**dagens ret**	*dayens rad*
starter	**forret**	*foh-red*
main course	**hovedret**	*hoh-veth-red*
dessert	**dessert**	*deh-seh'd*
wine list	**vinkort**	*veen-cod*
sweet	**sødt**	*sodt*
sour	**surt**	*suad*
spicy	**stærkt**	*stehgd*
May I have the bill?	**Må jeg bede om regningen?**	*moh yay beh-theh uhm rahy-ning-ehn*

Menu Decoder

agurk	*a-guag*	cucumber
ananas	*a-nah-nas*	pineapple
appelsin	*abbel-seen*	orange
blomme	*blum-ma*	plum
brød	*bruth*	bread
champignon	*sham-pee-ong*	mushroom
danskvand	*dansg vann*	mineral water
fersken	*fes-gehn*	peach
fisk	*fesgg*	fish
fløde	*flu-theh*	cream
gulerod	*gooleh-roth*	carrot
grøntsager	*grunn-saha*	vegetables
hummer	*humma*	lobster
is	*ees*	ice cream
kaffe	*kah-feh*	coffee
kartofler	*kah-toff-lah*	potatoes
kød	*kuth*	meat
kylling	*killing*	chicken
kål	*kohl*	cabbage
laks	*lahggs*	salmon
lam	*lahm*	lamb
leverpostej	*leh-vah-poh-stie*	liver paté
løg	*loy*	onion
mælk	*mailgg*	milk
oksekød	*ogg-seh-kuth*	beef
ost	*ossd*	cheese
peber	*peh-ba*	pepper
pore	*po-a*	leek
purløj	*poo-a-loy*	chives
pølse	*pill-seh*	sausage
rejer	*rah-yah*	shrimps
ris	*rees*	rice
rødspætte	*roth-speh-da*	plaice
røget fisk	*roy-heth fesgg*	smoked fish
saftevand	*sah-fteh-vann*	squash
salat	*sah-lad*	salad
salt	*sald*	salt
sild	*sil*	herring
skaldyr	*sgall-dya*	shellfish
skinke	*sgeng-geh*	ham
smør	*smuah*	butter
sodavand	*sodah-vann*	fizzy drink
steg	*stie*	steak
svinekød	*svee-neh-kuth*	pork
syltetøj	*sill-teh-toi*	jam
te	*teh*	tea
tærte	*te-ah-teh*	quiche/pie
torsk	*tohsgg*	cod
vand	*vann*	water

wienerbrød	*vee-nah-bryd*	Danish pastry
æble	*eh-bleh*	apple
æg	*egg*	egg
øl	*uhl*	beer

Time

today	**i dag**	*ee-day*
tomorrow	**i morgen**	*ee-mohn*
yesterday	**i går**	*ee-goh*
before noon	**formiddag**	*foh-medday*
afternoon	**eftermiddag**	*ehftah-medday*
evening	**aften**	*ahftehn*
night	**nat**	*nadd*
minute	**minut**	*meh-nude*
hour	**time**	*tee-meh*
week	**uge**	*oo-eh*
month	**måned**	*moe-neth*
year	**år**	*oah*

Days of the Week

Monday	**mandag**	*mann-day*
Tuesday	**tirsdag**	*teahs-day*
Wednesday	**onsdag**	*uns-day*
Thursday	**torsdag**	*toahs-day*
Friday	**fredag**	*frey-day*
Saturday	**lørdag**	*lur-day*
Sunday	**søndag**	*son-day*

Months

January	**januar**	*ya-nuah*
February	**februar**	*fib-buah*
March	**marts**	*mahds*
April	**april**	*apreal*
May	**maj**	*mai*
June	**juni**	*yoo-nee*
July	**juli**	*yoo-lee*
August	**august**	*auw-guhsd*
September	**september**	*sehb-tem-bah*
October	**oktober**	*ogg-toh-bah*
November	**november**	*noh-vem-bah*
December	**december**	*deh-sem-bah*

Numbers

0	**nul**	*noll*
1	**en**	*ehn*
2	**to**	*toh*
3	**tre**	*tray*
4	**fire**	*fee-ah*
5	**fem**	*femm*
6	**seks**	*seggs*
7	**syv**	*siu*
8	**otte**	*oh-deh*
9	**ni**	*nee*
10	**ti**	*tee*
20	**tyve**	*tyh-veh*
30	**tredive**	*traith-veh*
40	**fyrre**	*fyr-reh*
50	**halvtreds**	*hahl-traiths*
60	**tres**	*traiths*
70	**halvfjerds**	*hahl-fyads*
80	**firs**	*fee-ahs*
90	**halvfems**	*hahl-femms*
100	**hundrede**	*hoon-dreh-the*
200	**tohundrede**	*toh-hoon-dreh-the*
1,000	**tusind**	*tooh-sin-deh*
2,000	**totusinde**	*toh-tooh-sin-deh*

Selected Copenhagen Street Index